100 Minutes

Making Every Minute Count in the Literacy Block

Lisa Donohue

Pembroke Publishers Limited

© 2012 Pembroke Publishers
538 Hood Road
Markham, Ontario, Canada L3R 3K9
www.pembrokepublishers.com

Distributed in the U.S. by Stenhouse Publishers
480 Congress Street
Portland, ME 04101
www.stenhouse.com

We acknowledge the financial support of the Government of Canada through the Book Publishing Industry Development Program (BPIDP) for our publishing activities.

We acknowledge the assistance of the Government of Ontario through the Ontario Media Development Corporation's Ontario Book Initiative.

Library and Archives Canada Cataloguing in Publication

Donohue, Lisa
100 minutes : making every minute count in the literacy block / Lisa Donohue.

Includes bibliographical references and index.
Issued also in electronic format.
ISBN 978-1-55138-276-0

1. Literacy--Study and teaching (Elementary). 2. English language--Study and teaching (Elementary). 3. Language arts (Elementary). I. Title. II. Title: One hundred minutes.

LB1576.D65 2012   372.6'044   C2012-903955-1

eBook format ISBN 978-1-55138-845-8

Editor: Kat Mototsune
Cover Design: John Zehethofer
Typesetting: Jay Tee Graphics Ltd.

Printed and bound in Canada
9 8 7 6 5 4 3 2 1

MIX
Paper from
responsible sources
FSC® C004071

Contents

Introduction

This book is by far the most comprehensive look at literacy and learning that I have ever ventured to write. In the past, I have taken isolated elements of literacy and examined them in a detailed and thorough manner. However, the question I get asked the most frequently is this: "How do you fit it all in?"

When we begin to examine literacy, it is easy to be overwhelmed by the number of skills, strategies, and elements that fit under the umbrella of the term. In a regular instructional day, a typical literacy block contains approximately 100 minutes. But what exactly do we need to fit into that time? When we think of balanced literacy or comprehensive literacy, we think of all elements of literacy learning, including reading, writing, oral communication, and media literacy. But it goes well beyond these four subject areas.

Balanced literacy has referred to the use of the gradual release of responsibility in the teaching–learning cycle, including modelled reading, shared reading, guided reading, independent reading, modelled writing, guided writing, independent writing, and writing workshops. However, in order to truly balance literacy, we have to include much more than the basics of this teaching–learning cycle. Balancing literacy asks us to

- provide opportunities for students to think, talk, and share
- conference with small groups of students and individuals
- plan time for students to examine exemplars and model texts in order to create success criteria
- have students provide and receive feedback with their peers and teacher
- build in rich tasks, higher-order thinking, open-ended questions, and collaborative learning opportunities
- integrate technology by teaching students to analyze and create media works, and to think critically and analytically about the texts they encounter
- provide opportunities for students to have choice and voice in their learning, to capitalize on their own strengths, to identify areas for growth and set personal learning goals
- differentiate to ensure that all students are demonstrating their learning in ways that are meaningful and relevant to them
- integrate learning from other subject areas and find texts that students can connect to
- teach students to write in a variety of text forms, including fiction and nonfiction; to write for a variety of purposes and audiences; and to read and think critically
- encourage students to write with voice and passion

- use ongoing assessment to monitor and evaluate students' learning, and to guide our instruction
- accommodate students with different learning styles and modify for students with differing abilities
- foster a love for learning

It's no wonder that the challenge of "balancing the literacies" seems completely overwhelming—not to mention the reality of fitting it all into a limited amount of allotted literacy time.

Although literacy blocks can differ in length, it is possible to fit all of these important aspects into a 100-minute block. By chunking a literacy block into three distinct sections, it *is* possible to provide opportunities for students to engage in all aspects of literacy every week. With this model, it is possible to provide daily explicit instruction in both reading and writing, and to meet with every student on a regular basis for guided reading and writing conferences. It is possible to integrate technology, promote higher-order thinking, and engage students in their learning through tasks that provide choices. It is possible to form meaningful connections between the work that students are doing independently and the learning that is happening in other areas of literacy instruction. It is possible to build assessment right into the literacy block so that students receive immediate purposeful feedback. It is possible to do all of this, and keep your sanity…I promise!

Acknowledgments

As promised, this book is dedicated to the man who penned its title—Michael Cohen.

This book is a blend of new theory, existing classroom pedagogy, ongoing research, valuable sources, and trusted resources. There have been many people who have influenced and supported me along the way and I appreciate each and every one of them.

Thanks to Judy Spiers for taking the time to help me work things through and providing me with invaluable resources and advice. Through Learning Connections, Deb Kitchener enabled me to meet with a fabulous network of educators, whose support and ongoing spirit of collaboration has helped and inspired me greatly. Thanks to Jennifer Branch and David Booth, literacy leaders who helped me frame my thinking.

My personal learning networks—within my school board and extending beyond, face-to-face and through Twitter—have challenged me, enriched my experiences, and caused me to think about and rethink effective classroom practice. I highly value the times I spend working with literacy leaders, especially Royan Lee and Angie Harrison, and thank them for taking the time to write their contributions for this book. Farhana Panju and Nikki Town provided endless support, feedback, and cheerleading as this book began to take shape.

To my very trusted friends and partners at Pembroke—Mary Macchiusi and Kat Mototsune: Thanks for your patience, creativity, and ongoing assistance with everything *100 Minutes*, from the big things (like overall organization of the manuscript) to your attention to details (like creating the perfect icons).

Finally, a huge thanks to my family—Mike, Matthew, Hailey, and my dad—for putting up with my mental clutter and constant distractedness as I spent the last few years working on the various pieces of this book. I'm sure if we were to count it up, there would be hundreds of hours in 100 Minutes. Thanks for your patience, understanding, and love!

PART ONE

Finding the Balance

True Confessions of How I Spent My First 100 Minutes

I remember when I first began teaching 15 years ago. I sat every night staring at the vast chunk of time that was scheduled in my daybook for Language Arts: 100 minutes a day. That was 500 minutes a week, a total of 8 hours and 20 minutes of language instruction weekly. It was an immense chunk of time! Every night, I pored over the resources I had available to me. I had to find ways to fill that time. I knew that students needed to read, write, spell, and learn grammar. Those were the basics, the fundamentals I knew about at the time. I filled hour after hour, day after day, with reading activities, worksheets, independent writing, and spelling units. I knew that the writing process had multiple steps (pre-writing, drafting, writing, editing, and publishing), although I was unsure about how to help each child at each stage; I was always overwhelmed with the line that formed at my desk on the days students were editing their rough copies. I believed that everything students wrote needed to go through the whole writing process; therefore my students spent hours rewriting second drafts and final copies of their work.

As for reading, we read together. We read stories as a class, each child taking a turn to read out loud. I asked them simple questions and they answered them. In my classroom, we had a rule: One person speaks at a time. That was a sign of respect. The students followed along and responded by raising their hands. I even remember saying, "How can you learn if you're talking?" After reading, students would complete page after page of comprehension questions. I knew that I needed to monitor their comprehension but, to be honest, I didn't know what that truly was, let alone how to monitor it.

We had a spelling routine: every Monday I did a pre-test and every Friday we had the spelling test. Even then, I had the beginnings of understanding of the importance of diagnostic assessment; however, I wasn't sure what to do with the kids who already knew all the words so, in a feeble attempt at differentiation, those students were responsible for the regular spelling list as well as the "enrichment words." Only the students who had perfect spelling (or close to that) were rewarded with the prize of getting additional work. I thought that was what it meant to cater to the needs of all students.

Day after day, I filled my 100 minutes with reading, writing, spelling, and grammar work. Gradually, the busy routines of my language program seemed to fill the time. In fact, I was so successful filling the 100-minute literacy block that I found it difficult to always find time to read aloud to my students—a promise I made them at the beginning of every year. Although I didn't truly understand the importance of reading aloud, I knew it was something we all enjoyed, and it was good for 15 to 20 minutes of time a day.

Time passed, years went by. I settled into the busy routine of filling our days with language activities. I was doing the best I could but, for some reason, I knew it wasn't working for every child. I had no idea how to fix that.

One day, I was introduced to the idea of guided reading. Guided reading? Working with small groups of students on texts specifically chosen for the students' ability and interest? Impossible! There was no way that I would be able to work every day with a small group while the rest of the students were in the classroom. What a ridiculous concept. Why teach a reading lesson five times to individual groups of students, when I could teach it once to everyone? And what on earth would the rest of the kids be doing while I'm sitting with this one group of kids? I was certain that my classroom would erupt in total anarchy. And yet, something deep inside me assured me that this was the direction I needed to pursue. With the support of my teacher-librarian, I began to experiment with the concept of small-group instruction. My 100-minute literacy time was already full, and now it was becoming cramped. I had already filled my time with reading, writing, spelling and grammar activities, and now, I needed to include guided reading as well? What was I supposed to give up? Regardless, we eked out time in the daily 100 minutes for guided reading, as we played with this "new and innovative" teaching strategy.

More time passed, more years. Along came a new model for instruction and a new approach to teaching language. It was now called balanced literacy, and focused on the use of the gradual release of responsibility. In this new model, teachers were to gradually release the responsibility of learning to the students through a series of learning activities. First, the teacher would model the skill, then the students would practice with the support of the teacher, then the teacher would work with small groups (ah-ha! something I was already familiar with), and finally the students would work independently. However, this model added a whole new set of literacy routines to my 100 minutes. I now needed to include modelled reading (something I had often sacrificed in the effort to conserve time for more "purposeful" tasks), shared reading (of which I had no idea what it really was or how it worked), guided reading (an area I was becoming familiar with, but was far from an expert in), and independent reading (something I believed meant kids reading on their own for a sustained period of time). And the balanced literacy model also pertained to writing. This was something completely new for me. How could we use the gradual release of responsibility in writing too? Guided writing groups? Was there even such a thing? Modelled writing, shared writing, guided writing, independent writing—where were these to fit into my 100 minutes? Again, I went back to my list of language activities: reading, writing, spelling, and grammar. What did I need to sacrifice in order to fit in this new model?

Again, time passed. I began thinking about different aspects of literacy. I began wondering about how to help students make intentional connections between the things I was teaching and the things they were learning independently. I started to wonder about how to monitor their comprehension when they were reading independently. I questioned the authenticity of their tasks. I knew that I needed to provide some accountability to students to ensure that their independent reading time was purposeful and authentic; however, I didn't want to overwhelm them by making them write about everything they read. How could I monitor their independent work in ways that were effective and efficient? How could I do all of this and still keep my sanity?

And still more years went by. More and more got added to the demands of my 100 minutes. Now I had to include assessment for learning in the form of learning targets and success criteria; find opportunities for individual and peer conferences;

provide students with meaningful feedback based on their individual goals and the learning targets. I had to include choice. It seemed that every time I turned around more and more was being added to the demands of my time. Along came the new literacies—now I had to include digital literacy, media literacy, critical literacy, social literacy. And even more was added: target student engagement, foster autonomy, promote higher-order thinking, build in opportunities for accountable talk, make meaningful connections to other content areas and the world around us. Help raise global citizens who see the world as an interconnected place and understand that their classrooms may have walls but not boundaries. Help students connect, collaborate, create, and communicate both face-to-face, and through the use of digital tools. Use technology rather than teach technology. Build on the solid foundations of reading, writing, listening, and speaking. Teach students to evaluate, integrate, consolidate. The only thing that remained the same was that I still needed to accomplish this in 100 minutes of my day, 500 minutes a week, for a total of 8 hours and 20 minutes of literacy instruction every week. Now the time seemed hardly adequate. Was it even possible to balance all the things that the new balanced literacy demanded? How could I use 100 minutes of daily instruction to target such a vast array of learning?

1

100 Minutes to Balance Literacy

For the past three years, with the support of my teaching colleagues, I have explored a new model for a 100-minute literacy block. This model is based on the fundamental belief that students need time for explicit teaching, time for guided practice, and time for independent work. Students need to have choice in their learning and to have their individual voices heard. Technology should never be an additional thing to teach—nor should the new literacies—but instead should be an integrated component of daily instruction. Higher-order thinking can be fostered through the vehicle of accountable talk. And, most importantly, students should always see their learning as important, relevant, and authentic. Although the demands of literacy instruction today are far more complex than they were when I first started teaching, the use of a simple three-part framework can make it possible for all students to engage in all of the essential components of literacy, to make meaningful connections between the things they are learning through instruction and independent practice, and to have frequent opportunities for feedback, goal-setting, and ongoing assessment. This model builds in opportunities for accountable talk, higher-order thinking, and collaboration.

As teachers, we want a framework for learning that maximizes every minute we spend with our students; a model that provides simple strategies for differentiation and includes choice; a model that seamlessly integrates digital literacy, critical thinking, higher-order thinking, accountable talk, media literacy; a model that provides teachers with the opportunity to meet the needs of all students; a model that does it all in 100 minutes.

What Does *Balanced* Mean?

As we begin to think of ways to best utilize the daily block of 100 minutes, we need to truly understand what balanced literacy means. We are now well into the 21st century, and yet this term is still used as if it referred to the "cutting edge." The reality is that most of the students we are teaching were born in this century and know no other. The concept of anything other than the 21st century is ancient history to our youngsters. This means that the world they were born into is vastly different from the world in which many of us went to school. These are kids who use digital tools in ways that we used the phone. They use online resources in the way we might have used the old World Book encyclopedia. They question, they click, they find. They are not limited by their physical spaces; when given the opportunity they will explore online media the way we used to thumb through magazines. As the definition of literacy expands to encompass the realities of the current generation, so too must our understanding of balanced literacy.

As I reflect on my journey to understand literacy in a broader sense, it becomes clear that it needs to include the multi-literacies that are a part of our students' lives outside school. Does that mean we disregard all of the work that came before? Does that mean that the previous definitions of balanced literacy are no longer relevant? I don't think so. I believe that the term *balanced literacy* now needs to include not only the fundamentals of reading, writing, listening, and speaking, but also the model of instruction (including modelled, shared, guided, and independent learning opportunities) and the vehicle through which we learn and communicate (print and online texts, digital tools, media texts, collaborative learning, critical thinking).

A balanced literacy program means much more than just providing opportunities for students to participate in reading and writing in a single day. In the 21st century, we must not only provide a balanced literacy program, but we must also balance the literacies in new ways. We need to think, not only about the elements of literacy, but of all the literacies—the old literacies and the new. Balancing the literacies means much more than maintaining a schedule for literacy instruction on a daily basis.

While students need routines, and routines are necessary for all students to be successful, without constant revisiting routines become mundane, boring, and monotonous. I'm not saying that we should abandon routines; in fact, nothing could be further from the truth. The only way to build independence is with consistent routines. However, these routines need to continue to deepen and become richer as the year progresses. Students need to add layers to their routines, adding choices and deepening their experiences.

As we flesh out these different components of a literacy block, we begin to balance all the things our students need. We balance their experiences not only from one day to the next, but subsequently from week to week, and ultimately from month to month through the year. It is the growing sophistication, or deepening, of the tasks that allows students to continue their learning and broaden their thinking. By establishing strong consistent routines and then not only maintaining them but enriching them, we are able to create a truly dynamic literacy time in which all students are able to engage in a wide variety of rich learning tasks.

If we were to try to teach each of these elements of the new balanced literacy in isolation, we would certainly need more than 100 minutes a day. In fact, there would probably not be enough hours in the entire school day to address all these areas independently. However, through the use of three intentionally crafted blocks of time, we can build literacy routines that balance the literacies from day to day, week to week, and ultimately through the year.

If teaching were like cooking, we'd be able to consistently follow a recipe, or a prescribed set of steps, and successfully teach every student, every year. It would be comforting to know that if we completed a given checklist of literary experiences we'd be fulfilling the requirement of teaching literacy in a balanced way. Although there are elements of literacy that are essential to include every day, once routines become stale and mundane student engagement quickly decreases. The challenge we face as educators is to find a way of enriching routines and adding to them over time in such a way that students are able to select from a wide variety of activities within familiar routines.

When we build a literacy block, we need to begin with a solid foundation. That foundation is based on the simple routines of the core elements of the block. These elements remain essentially the same throughout the year, but continue to be the framework that holds all the other pieces in place. As the year progresses, we need to add new layers to our block; each layer brings a new level of complexity and sophistication. As we add to our students' literary experiences, we need to ensure that we are fostering independence at each level. Each new experience brings with it a new set of learning goals and expectations. We need to make sure that, as we introduce our students to these new layers, we are taking the time necessary to ensure that they are confident with not only the routines, but also the learning targets each new experience brings. Taking the time to introduce students to all tasks, modelling sample work, and co-constructing success criteria will ensure that everyone shares a common understanding of the expectations of all tasks.

Building a literacy block takes time. There is no way that students can begin a school year in the fall and immediately jump into rich, differentiated, independent and shared learning experiences in all areas of literacy. That becomes our goal over time. As students begin to develop a comfort level with the expectations we have set for them, we know it is time to begin to add another layer to our instruction. There is a fine balance between fostering routines and creating monotony. Bored students are disengaged students, and their level of performance is reduced. Doing the same thing day after day, week after week, month after month, is a formula that would certainly result in student fatigue and lack of interest. However, if we add new dimensions to these familiar routines, we encourage students to see them in fresh new ways; then the routines can serve as a comfortable framework on which they are able to build new learning experiences.

100 ÷ 3 = A Balanced Literacy Block

"Literacy is the ability to use language and images in rich and varied forms to read, write, listen, speak, view, represent and think critically about ideas. It enables us to share information, to interact with others, and make meaning. Literacy is a complex process that involves building on prior knowledge, culture and experiences in order to develop new knowledge and deeper understanding. It connects individuals and communities, and is an essential tool for personal growth and active participation in a democratic society." —Ontario Ministry of Education (2004)

The key to forming a basic framework for a literacy block that can effectively meet all the requirements of a truly balanced literacy program is to divide it into blocks of time. Within these blocks of time, it is possible for teachers to provide daily whole-class instruction in both reading and writing, as well as daily small-group instruction. Students are able to engage in a wide range of independent and collaborative learning activities that are directly connected to their learning. Teachers are able to monitor and provide immediate feedback on students' work, assisting them in setting realistic goals that will continue to drive their learning forward. By creating flexible chunks of time within the literacy block, we are able to teach in ways that are responsive to our students' needs but remain firmly grounded in the learning targets and expectations for each group of students.

The 100 Minutes literacy framework is comprised of three distinct blocks of time. Two of these provide time for direct instruction in reading and writing; the third allows time for students to work independently or in small groups. As students work independently, they are applying their writing and reading on a daily basis: hence the term AWARD Time (Applying Writing And Reading Daily). During direct-instruction Reading Time and Writing Time, teachers are able to explicitly teach students about the various skills associated with reading and writing; during AWARD Time, students are able to apply this learning to their own work. AWARD Time presents valuable opportunities for the teacher to conference with small groups of students for reading and writing.

This framework provides embedded opportunities for students to learn, practice, and apply new skills through the gradual release of responsibility. In this model the teacher introduces the students to new learning through modelling and direct instruction. Then, through guided instruction, the teacher is able to support, monitor, and provide feedback to students as they begin to apply and integrate their new learning. Finally, students are able to work on their own in order to use this new learning independently. According to Pearson and Gallagher (1983), effective literacy instruction depends on the teacher providing scaffolded support to help each student develop beyond his/her current level of achievement, while gradually releasing responsibility to the student to facilitate independent learning. In order for students to acquire new literacy skills and strengthen existing ones, the teacher needs to begin by modelling effective strategies; then using small-group instruction as a vehicle for coaching, guiding, and providing feedback; supporting students as they begin to practice new skills; and finally building in opportunities for students to work independently to apply their new learning.

By including two chunks of time for whole-group instruction and one chunk of time for students to engage in independent shared and guided learning experiences, the 100 Minutes framework provides opportunities for the gradual release of responsibility to be seamlessly integrated into all literacy experiences. As students transition from large-group to small-group instruction and then to independent work, they are introduced to new skills, guided through them, and finally encouraged to practice and apply them.

The Basics

Each chunk of time in a 100 Minutes literacy block can be used for a variety of purposes, and the instructional content will broaden and change as the year progresses. However, for simplicity's sake, we'll start with the basics.

Reading Time: Imagine the first chunk of time as a 20- to 30-minute whole-class lesson. This time could be used for direct instruction in reading. This is the time when the teacher would introduce reading comprehension strategies, model thinking while reading, pose higher-order–thinking questions, and encourage students to talk with each other about the texts. During this time, the teacher might also choose to introduce different reading responses, model sample responses, and set learning goals with students about their reading.

AWARD Time: The second chunk is a slightly longer period of time—approximately 40 minutes—when students would have the opportunity to work independently, collaboratively, or in small groups on a wide range of tasks. These could include independent reading, responding to reading, independent writing, accessing technology, media study, word skills, and opportunities for sharing with peers and for giving and receiving feedback. While students are working on these tasks, the teacher would have the opportunity to meet with at least two groups of students (for 15 to 20 minutes each). This time could be spent on guided reading, writing conferences, or any other lesson for which students might need small-group direct instruction.

Writing Time: The third and final chunk of time, another block of 20 to 30 minutes, could be used for whole-class instruction again, this time with a focus on writing. The teacher could use this time to introduce new forms of writing; model writing; create success criteria with students; have students engage in collaborative writing activities; explicitly teach writing skills, such as descriptive writing, writing with voice, writing for an audience, word usage, and figurative language; teach grammar and sentence fluency; and much more.

You will notice that the durations of the elements are varied and flexible. Within this suggested framework, flexibility is paramount. As all learners are different, so are all classes. While a longer instructional time works for one group of learners, it might need to be shortened for another. Some learners thrive during the independent work time, whereas others might need to move quickly from one activity to another in order to remain engaged. As with all instructional frameworks, teachers should consider these strategies as suggestions rather than hard and fast rules. As teachers get to know their learners, they should adjust their literacy routines in ways that best meet their students' needs. Teachers should be one part artist, one part scientist, one part psychologist, and one part gymnast—remember that flexibility is always the greatest gift we can give ourselves and our students. I remember my mother—a teacher herself—quoting an old proverb: "Blessed are the flexible, for they shall not be bent out of shape."

100 Minutes in Action

The first day of school is an overwhelming experience for us all. I don't think any teacher, regardless of how long they've been teaching, ever loses those first-day butterflies.

Imagine standing at the front of your class on the first day. As you look at the anxious sun-kissed faces of the students, they stare back with an intense gaze. Their eyes seem to search yours, and a slightly uncomfortable silence falls across the room. The students giggle nervously; their excitement is palpable. You get a feeling that this moment is too profound and important to lose. There is the need to say something momentous, something earth-shattering, something really, really important. But nothing comes to mind. You recognize that you are all about to begin a year-long journey together. You wonder how you will ever learn everything you need to know about these youngsters in your care and, in fact, at this moment you'd settle for knowing their names. In just a short few months, you'll know these learners in profound ways. You'll know their strengths, needs, wants, and desires. You'll know the names of their pets and the places they go on vacation. You'll recognize them by their voices, their writing, and, for some, even their coughs and sneezes. What a momentous day, the start of a tremendous journey. Perhaps you begin your time together by reading a favorite story or asking the students to write about themselves; maybe you play a simple getting-to-know-you game. Regardless, it is the start of something great!

Flash forward a few months.

As the bell rings, students enter your class with a sense of excitement and eagerness. Each quickly finds a spot on the carpet beside a talking-partner. Before you begin, you frame a story with a Big Thinking Question. Students pause a moment to give it some thought. You read aloud, pausing occasionally to pose a question or two or to model your thinking. Students share their ideas with their talk-partners and every child has a chance to know that his/her voice has been heard. You finish reading and provide students a few moments to reflect on the Big Thinking Question before asking them to talk one more time. You might record some responses in writing, or perhaps just engage in a thoughtful conversation with the students.

Next, students begin to work independently or collaboratively. They all seem to go in different directions at once, all busying themselves with important tasks. Some pick up their books, some take out their reading responses, others head off to a computer or digital device. A few peruse the classroom library and a couple work on their writing: making changes to something they had previously written or starting something new. The transition takes only a few minutes as the students gather the necessary resources and begin their work. This is your opportunity to meet with a small group of students for direct instruction.

After a focused guided-reading lesson with a group, you give all students a signal to change to their second activity. In the next moments, students transition to a new learning task, taking the time only to finish a sentence, idea, or paragraph. You meet with another group of students: reflecting on their personal writing goals and a piece of recent writing. As you focus your attention on one student at the table, two others automatically begin to share with each other, eager to discuss their work and valuing the opinions and feedback from their classmates. In a few minutes, you have had the opportunity to conference with each child in the group; they have reflected on their writing and determined a goal that they will continue to work on.

You realize that you still have a few minutes to check in with a student who has been struggling with his reading. You meet with him quietly at his desk, sharing a moment or two reading together. You again signal the students to finish up their tasks, asking them to meet you on the carpet in a few minutes.

The students gather again on the carpet. You use this opportunity to introduce a new form of writing. You begin by providing pairs of students with different samples of writing and asking them to put them in an order that shows the weakest to strongest pieces of writing. Working with their talk-partners, they disperse into the classroom, engaging in conversations about what is present and missing from the various pieces of writing. Perhaps a heated debate breaks out as to which sample the students believe is the strongest piece of writing. You listen as they argue passionately about why one piece is better than the other, justifying their views by pointing out features in the writing. You hear, "This one has spelling mistakes, it can't be the best," while another students says, "Yeah, but the ideas are really good and listen to the way the writer described them." In a short time, the students have reached their decisions and either agreed or agreed to disagree. They reassemble on the carpet and you begin a discussion with them that is framed around the question "What did the strong samples have that the weak ones did not?" As students share their observations, you record these as ideas to keep in mind when students are working on their own writing.

Before you know it, the bell is sounding again and 100 minutes of your day has passed.

How is it possible that in just a few short months your classroom has become such a rich environment for student learning? How is it possible that students are able to monitor their own learning, set goals for themselves, and provide feedback to each other? How is it possible that after such a short time you've not only learned their names, but you've come to know so much more about every single learner? Where will you go next? How will you maintain the momentum and creativity that's alive and humming in the classroom? How can you continue to challenge? Enrich? Differentiate? Support? Engage? Excite? Motivate? You understand that balanced literacy means more than a routine of activities, but it is through the establishment of routines that you are able to truly address all the things you need to in order to balance all the literacies. Day to day, month to month, 100 minutes at a time.

2

The Building Blocks

At the beginning of a new year, it is important to set the tone that will carry through the remainder of the year. By taking the time to establish a strong literacy routine, you can ensure that students are engaged in meaningful learning in all aspects of literacy. Students need to have a clear understanding of the various elements of the daily literacy routine.

A Framework of Direct Instruction

The first elements to introduce into a literacy block should be the times dedicated to whole-class direct instruction. These times bookend the literacy block, comprising the beginning and the end of the 100 minutes. Most teachers have a selection of community-building activities they choose to introduce at the beginning of the year, from playing games to determining a class set of agreements. These activities are highly valuable in establishing a positive climate and a sense of community for students. Using the literacy block for some of these activities is an option.

It is possible to introduce students to these first two elements of the literacy block, even on the first day of school. By carving out some time on either end of the literacy block, you can begin to set up the routines that will be foundational for the remainder of the year. You might start a literacy block with Reading Time consisting of a whole-class reading lesson, such as reading a book aloud to students. Posing a few thoughtful questions to students can gain you a little insight into the group of learners as a whole. In the first few days of school, this will be a time you can use for reading aloud to students and beginning to actively teach them how they can engage in conversations with each other.

Likewise, ending the literacy block with a Writing Time consisting of whole-class writing instruction sets the tone for a positive, focused learning environment. For example, in the beginning days of school you might model a writing task, such as writing a letter to the students, creating a class contract of agreements, or even reflecting on the summer. Whatever the content, the students will be introduced to the way the time will be used for focused direct instruction.

As time goes on, these two blocks of time will form the foundation for all whole-class literacy instruction. It will be a time to introduce students to forms of writing and to model reading strategies. It will be a time when students will learn to apply critical thinking skills and brainstorm potential topics for writing. It will be the foundational component of direct instruction in which you actively teach the big ideas of the literacy curriculum.

"The same approaches to teaching and learning apply in all literacy programs for all students....They include a strong oral language component, scaffolding on prior knowledge and experiences, and a focus on higher-order thinking and critical literacy practices."— Ontario Ministry of Education (2004: 7)

Why Direct Instruction Is Important

In whole-class learning experiences, the teacher explicitly teaches effective literacy strategies. It is a time when the teacher can demonstrate thinking aloud in order for students to become aware of what happens in a reader's head when that person is reading and thinking about texts. This time can be used for introducing students to new text forms and purposes for writing, or for considering various audiences for writing. The teacher can use this time for mini-lessons in grammar and word skills, ensuring that these remain grounded in authentic reading and writing experiences. Through whole-class experiences, students explore higher-order thinking questions by engaging in discussions about texts. It is a time when teachers can pose open-ended questions and encourage students to think, question, share, explore, and justify their ideas. It is a time when teachers can introduce new skills to the group of learners as a whole.

You might find this chart helpful when building the literacy block. When you take the time to establish the various literacy elements in a logical sequential way, students are able to use the times to maximize their learning—in a whole-class group, in a small guided group, or working independently. In the first week or two of school, organizing your literacy block in the following way will provide a foundation for future elements.

THE LITERACY BLOCK: INTRODUCING DIRECT INSTRUCTION

Approximate time	Literacy Activity	
15–30 minutes	Direct Instruction: Reading Time	
	Teacher	Students
	Modelled Reading Teaching students how to engage with texts by reading aloud, explicitly teaching reading strategies, posing higher-order thinking questions, etc.	**Whole Class** Active participation in reading lesson.
	Teacher-selected community-building activities	
15–30 minutes	Direct Instruction: Writing Time	
	Teacher	Students
	Writing Instruction Teaching students various writing skills through modelling, examination of mentor texts, establishing success criteria, etc.	**Whole Class** Active participation in writing lessons.

Building In Independence

As early as the first week of school, teachers can begin to introduce students to independent learning routines. These two independent routines—independent reading and independent writing—require stamina-building and will take days, if not weeks, to successfully establish. Patience and consistency are the keys to developing these essential elements. Independent reading time and independent writing time are when students will practice, transfer, and apply the learning that takes place in all other areas of the literacy block. You need to establish clear, consistent expectations for these times to enable all students to focus on their own learning.

The time that is invested in the first weeks of school to set the stage for focused independent learning will be very much valued as the year progresses. Independent work times make it possible for all small-group instruction to happen. It is essential that these two independent routines be firmly established in the beginning weeks of school. There may be times throughout the year when the expectations that are set at the beginning of the year are revisited in order to ensure that students continue to use their independent work times in a way that maximizes their learning and the learning of others.

Within the first few weeks of school, the literacy block should be starting to take shape, including four basic elements that combine direct instruction and independent practice in both reading and writing. This chart may be helpful when organizing a literacy block containing these four elements.

In all charts, repeated elements in the charts are shaded. New elements are marked with an asterisk.

THE LITERACY BLOCK: INTRODUCING INDEPENDENT LEARNING

Approximate time	Literacy Activity	
15–30 minutes	Direct Instruction: Reading Time	
	Teacher	Students
	Modelled Reading Teaching students how to engage with texts by reading aloud, explicitly teaching reading strategies, posing higher-order thinking questions, etc.	**Whole Class** Active participation in reading lesson.
10–15 minutes	Independent Reading *	
	Teacher	Students
	Once initial routine is established, this time can be used for completing independent reading assessments.	**Independent Reading** Reading a variety of texts on their own.
15–30 minutes	Direct Instruction: Writing Time	
	Teacher	Students
	Writing Instruction Teaching students various writing skills through modelling, examination of mentor texts, establishing success criteria, etc.	**Whole Class** Active participation in writing lessons.

10–20 minutes	Independent Writing *	
	Teacher	Students
	Once the initial routine is established, this time can be used for independent reading/ writing assessments.	**Independent Writing** Working on their writing independently.

Incorporating Choice

Although choice is an important element in student learning, we are ultimately responsible for providing options and guiding the students with our decisions. Incorporating choice does not mean that the students are in total control; it means that they are able to partner with the teacher to make choices within a given set of parameters.

When we incorporate choice into student learning, research has shown that student engagement and achievement increases. Amosa et al (2008) concluded that tasks that allow students to demonstrate their learning in a variety of ways score higher in intellectual quality, quality learning, and overall quality teaching. They also found that tasks scaffolded with clear instruction and a framework for learning, followed by creative tasks that were personally relevant for students, also score significantly higher.

Choice can be woven into a literacy block in many different ways. Students can be provided time to work on a literacy activity of their choice and allowed to choose which area of literacy they would like to work on (reading, writing, media, etc); or students might choose how they would like to demonstrate their learning within one area of literacy (e.g., a writing topic, a reading response, or a media form that would best convey their message).

Opportunities for students to choose can be embedded in all learning opportunities, with students being encouraged to choose the best way to represent their learning in all aspects of literacy, while the teacher oversees or facilitates the choices they are making; i.e., the teacher chooses *what* the student is learning, and the students choose *how* they are learning it. For example, one group of students might be working on demonstrating their responding to reading following a guided lesson on inferring. The teacher will have provided different responses that the students choose from in order to apply their learning. Another group could be working on writing for the purpose of persuading their audience, and they might have a selection of HOT (Higher-Order Thinking) Topics to choose from, making their writing personally relevant for them.

In this fashion, the teacher and students are able to work together to ensure that all learning goals are being met, and the students have choice in how they are practicing and demonstrating their learning. This allows for a constant integration of students' choice into their learning, while the teacher can orchestrate a routine that ensures a balance of all aspects of literacy. This ensures that students are participating in all learning opportunities on a regular basis, instead of self-selecting their favorite literacy activities while neglecting other less desirable tasks. When choice is embedded within each activity, students are able to select how they would like to learn the skills that the teacher requires them to learn.

Building In Small-Group Instruction

Once the independent routines have been established, it becomes possible to introduce students to small-group instruction. Small-group instruction is the heart and soul of the literacy block. It is the time when you can monitor

See page 122 for more on instructional grouping.

individual student learning, provide immediate feedback, and assist students in setting personal learning goals.

You might begin by forming learning groups with which to begin guided reading and writing conferences. At this point, the foundations to the literacy block are starting to take shape. You are starting to see the various elements of literacy instruction in place—including modelled reading, guided reading, independent reading, modelled writing, writing conferences, and independent writing.

Once students are comfortable working independently, the teacher can begin to use this time to meet with individual students or small groups of students. The students will start to become more familiar with the expectation that they need to work independently while the teacher works with small groups. By revisiting these norms and frequent reinforcement of students who are working well independently, it will be possible to now have a literacy block where independent reading and writing create opportunities for guided reading and writing.

Instructional Groupings

Students can be grouped in a variety of different ways in order to facilitate their learning. These groupings could include mixed-ability groups, talk-partners, instructional-level groupings, groupings by interest or topic, or self-selected partners. Instructional groupings can change according to the learning goals, the needs of the students, or the task itself. Students need to work with a variety of different partners and groups in order to strengthen their collaborative skills and learn from the ideas of others. As students are organized into various groupings throughout the literacy block, the teacher and students can make many decisions that affect the way that students are grouped. Flexibility and variety are the keys to success with student groupings.

This chart might be helpful when pacing out the literacy block as these new elements are added.

THE LITERACY BLOCK: INTRODUCING SMALL-GROUP INSTRUCTION

Approximate time	Literacy Activity	
15–30 minutes	Direct Instruction: Reading Time	
	Teacher	Students
	Modelled Reading Teaching students how to engage with texts by reading aloud, explicitly teaching reading strategies, posing higher-order thinking questions, etc.	**Whole Class** Active participation in reading lesson.

10–15 minutes	Independent Reading	
	Teacher	Students
	Guided Reading * Working with a small group of students to read a teacher-selected text.	**Independent Reading** Reading a variety of texts on their own.
15–30 minutes	Direct Instruction: Writing Time	
	Teacher	Students
	Writing Instruction Teaching students various writing skills through modelling, examination of mentor texts, establishing success criteria, etc.	**Whole Class** Active participation in writing lessons.
10-20 minutes	Independent Writing	
	Teacher	Students
	Writing Conferences * Working with a small group of students to share and provide feedback about their writing.	**Independent Writing** Working on their writing independently.

Constructing AWARD Time

At this point, students might be grouped into four flexible learning groups. These groups could be based on the teacher's initial observations of the students' learning strengths, needs, or interests. While these groups will be helpful in getting students into a literacy routine that flows smoothly from one learning task to another, students need to be aware that these groupings are only temporary and will be changed frequently.

At this point in the building of the literacy block, students have developed an understanding of the various expectations for different independent tasks. It becomes possible to cluster these independent times to provide a greater block of time in which students can work with the teacher and then transfer and apply their learning. In this way, some students might attend a guided reading session first, and then spend time working on their independent reading, which would give them an opportunity to transfer and apply the skills that they have just learned. Similarly, some students could begin with independent work time and then have a chance to share their writing with a teacher for a writing conference. It is this kind of intentionality in the sequencing of tasks that sets AWARD (Applying Writing And Reading Daily) Time apart from other literacy frameworks. Structuring a literacy block so that students are able to meet with the teacher immediately before reading independently and immediately following independent writing allows for timely instruction, feedback, and transfer of learning.

Students can be organized into groups in order to easily support the transitioning from one task to the other. While some tasks, such as Guided Reading and Writing Conference, would be completed while students are working in a group, the remainder of tasks would be completed independently.

The transition to AWARD Time might take students a while to become familiar with, but rest assured that the time that has already been invested in establishing independent routines will pay off now. You will need to give students a signal to know when to stop one independent task and begin another. This may be as simple as saying, "Take a few minutes to finish up your first task, and get ready to begin your next one."

Now the foundations of differentiation are in place. Students will be working on different tasks at different times, and you will begin to be able to tailor small-group instruction to suit individual student needs.

The following chart may help when chunking independent work times in order to form AWARD Time. Note that this chart is arranged to chronologically represent the entire literacy block, instead of separating independent reading and independent writing times.

THE LITERACY BLOCK: INTRODUCING AWARD TIME

Approximate time	Literacy Activity	
15–30 minutes	Direct Instruction: Reading Time	
	Teacher	Students
	Modelled Reading Teaching students how to engage with texts by reading aloud, explicitly teaching reading strategies, posing higher-order thinking questions, etc.	**Whole Class** Active participation in reading lesson.
30–40 minutes (divided into two 15–20 minute work times)	**AWARD Time ***	
	Teacher	Students
	Guided Reading – Group 1	**Group 1** – Guided Reading * **Group 2** – Independent Reading **Group 3** – Independent Writing **Group 4** – Independent Writing
	Writing Conference – Group 3	**Group 1** – Independent Reading **Group 2** – Independent Writing **Group 3** – Writing Conference * **Group 4** – Independent Reading
15–30 minutes	Direct Instruction: Writing Time	
	Teacher	Students
	Writing Instruction Teaching students various writing skills through modelling, examination of mentor texts, establishing success criteria, etc.	**Whole Class** Active participation in writing lessons.

Tracking AWARD Time

While all other elements remain the same on the following day, the tasks that students complete during AWARD Time will begin to rotate. Students are divided

See page 34 for the Tracking Board template, and page 35 for reproducible routine cards to use with your tracking board. Enlarge the Tracking Board as you copy it, making sure it is visible for all students in the classroom.

into groups as an organizational strategy. They don't complete all their activities as a group; rather, each group is assigned a different task (e.g., Group 1 works on Independent Reading while Group 2 has Tech Time). While some tasks, such as Peer Sharing, require collaboration, Word Skills and Independent Reading and Writing require students to work independently.

A class tracking board can be a very useful device to organize the four tasks and keep track as the remaining elements of the literacy block are added. Enlarge the template on page 34 and use copies of the routine cards on page 35, moving them around on your tracking board.

When you introduce students to AWARD Time, it requires that they take a great deal of responsibility for tracking their tasks. A tracking board can provide students with visual reminders of what they need to be doing during AWARD Time. For example, students in Group 1 are able to see that on the first day they meet with the teacher for Guided Reading and then they work on their Independent Reading. By moving the tasks down one spot on the tracking board, you can assign tasks for the following day. Three sequential days are given here, showing how each group would rotate through the various tasks.

Your tracking boards might look something like this:

The tracking charts for AWARD Time combine Word Skills and Peer Sharing for students after a Writing Conference. This indicates to students that they have a choice of activity: they can either have a Peer Conference or work on Word Skills, as both logically follow a Writing Conference.

SAMPLE TRACKING BOARD: DAY 1

Group	First I will…	Then I will…
Group 1	GUIDED READING	INDEPENDENT READING
Group 2	INDEPENDENT READING	INDEPENDENT WRITING
Group 3	INDEPENDENT WRITING	WRITING CONFERENCE
Group 4	INDEPENDENT WRITING	INDEPENDENT READING

By rotating the tasks down one cell every day, the individual task assignments are adjusted for the following day.

SAMPLE TRACKING BOARD: DAY 2

Group	First I will…	Then I will…
Group 1	INDEPENDENT WRITING	INDEPENDENT READING
Group 2	GUIDED READING	INDEPENDENT READING
Group 3	INDEPENDENT READING	INDEPENDENT WRITING
Group 4	INDEPENDENT WRITING	WRITING CONFERENCE

SAMPLE TRACKING BOARD: DAY 3

Group	First I will…	Then I will…
Group 1	INDEPENDENT WRITING	WRITING CONFERENCE
Group 2	INDEPENDENT WRITING	INDEPENDENT READING
Group 3	GUIDED READING	INDEPENDENT READING
Group 4	INDEPENDENT READING	INDEPENDENT WRITING

Building In Accountability

As the literacy block continues to develop, it becomes possible to add the elements that provide opportunities for ongoing monitoring of students' learning during their independent work times. Through these elements, teachers are able to assess students' reading comprehension, track the texts students are reading, and provide support and practice for students in specific learning areas. They can also include opportunities for peer conferencing and begin to integrate technology and media. Teachers can use direct-instruction Reading and Writing Times to introduce students to additional elements as they are added to the literacy routine. These elements include reading response, word skills, peer sharing, and technology (if possible).

If it has not already happened, this would be an appropriate time to form new learning groups. AWARD Time differs from other independent routines in that it allows the teacher to intentionally sequence the different tasks that the students will complete in order to maximize their learning. The AWARD tracking schedule shown here allows for students to immediately transfer learning from guided instruction to independent work, as well as to receive immediate feedback on work that is completed independently.

The student tracking chart might be helpful when building AWARD Time. The optional fifth group allows for students to use the entire independent learning time to complete technology-based tasks.

While the remainder of the literacy framework will stay the same, the AWARD Time can now be expanded to include Reading Response, Word Skills, Peer Sharing, and Tech Time.

SAMPLE TRACKING OF DETAILED AWARD TIME: DAY 1

Group	First I will...	Then I will...
Group 1	INDEPENDENT WRITING	WORD SKILLS / PEER SHARING
Group 2	INDEPENDENT WRITING	WRITING CONFERENCE
Group 3	INDEPENDENT READING	READING RESPONSE
Group 4	GUIDED READING	READING RESPONSE

| Group 5 | TECH TIME | TECH TIME |

SAMPLE TRACKING OF DETAILED AWARD TIME: DAY 2

Group	First I will...	Then I will...
Group 1	TECH TIME	TECH TIME
Group 2	INDEPENDENT WRITING	WORD SKILLS / PEER SHARING
Group 3	INDEPENDENT WRITING	WRITING CONFERENCE
Group 4	INDEPENDENT READING	READING RESPONSE
Group 5	GUIDED READING	READING RESPONSE

Again, when the tasks are rotated down one position, the students are able to continue to transfer their learning the following day. For example, students who met for guided reading and then worked on a reading-response task related to the text will have an opportunity the following day to read independently and transfer this learning to their independent reading texts. Students who spent time writing independently and then received feedback through a writing conference will have time the following day to revisit their writing and apply feedback by revising their work or applying it to a new piece of writing; they will then have an opportunity to share this writing with their peers or further strengthen word skills that might have been noted from their writing conference the previous day. The final optional group working on technology will realistically need the entire independent work time in order to access and best utilize the technology tools that are available. It is important to remember that all learning should be authentic and purposeful, and technology should never be used as a "busy" station for students.

Checking In

One final addition you might consider adding is a check-in at the end of AWARD Time. This short 10- to 15-minute period can provide an opportunity for you to monitor specific students or even meet with an additional guided group for some extra attention. During this time, you can encourage students to choose a literacy activity they would like to spend some additional time working on. With younger students, you might need to use shorter blocks of time, which would allow for more opportunities for guided instruction.

Building Blocks in Place

Here is the final literacy block:

THE LITERACY BLOCK

Approximate time	Literacy Activity			
15–30 minutes	Direct Instruction: Reading Time			
	Teacher	Students		
	Modelled Reading Teaching students how to engage with texts by reading aloud, explicitly teaching reading strategies, posing higher-order thinking questions, etc.	**Whole Class** Active participation in modelled reading lesson.		
30–40 minutes (divided into two 15–20 minute work times)	AWARD Time			
	Teacher	Students		
	Guided Reading – Group 4	Group	First I will…	Then I will…
		Group 1		

Writing Conference – Group 2	Group 2	INDEPENDENT WRITING · WRITING CONFERENCE
	Group 3	INDEPENDENT READING · READING RESPONSE
	Group 4	GUIDED READING · READING RESPONSE
	Group 5 (optional)	TECH TIME

Optional 10–15 minutes	**Optional** Check-in with individual students or additional guided reading lesson.	Student choice of learning task.
15–30 minutes	**Direct Instruction: Writing Time**	
	Teacher	Students
	Writing Instruction Teaching students various writing skills through modelling, examination of mentor texts, establishing success criteria, etc.	**Whole Class** Active participation in writing lessons.

At this point, all of the elements of the literacy block are firmly in place. By introducing students to each element in turn and taking time to build a literacy block, you set the stage for effective literacy instruction. You might find the overview of the process on page 33 helpful when planning daily and weekly literacy instruction.

Approximate timeline	Elements of Literacy Block
Week 1	• Begin by book-ending the literacy block with two distinct times for direct instruction, beginning with Reading Time and ending with Writing Time.
Weeks 2–3	• Add times for independent reading and writing, gradually increasing the time that students spend engaged in each task. • Begin to use independent work times to meet with individual students for reading assessments or initial observations.
Weeks 4–6	• Form initial instructional groupings and begin to use AWARD Time to conduct guided reading lessons and writing conferences, meeting with one group for guided reading during independent reading time and another group for a writing conference during independent writing time. • Introduce students to the tracking board, including literacy tasks to be completed during simplified AWARD Time: Independent Reading, Guided Reading, Independent Writing, Writing Conference. • Use direct-instruction Reading and Writing Times to introduce students to reading responses, peer sharing, and technology. At this point, it is best to keep it simple and include a limited selection of reading responses and a simple technology task; e.g., writing a book recommendation for a friend or reading a specific text from an online source.
Week 7+	• Add additional elements to AWARD tracking board, ensuring that students transition from one learning task to another in a way that intentionally connects independent learning tasks to small-group learning opportunities: e.g., Reading Response follows Guided Reading; Writing Conference follows Independent Writing. • Have students rotate through a 4- or 5-day cycle, completing 2–3 learning tasks a day. • Continue to revisit routines and expectations for all learning times, ensuring that students are having opportunities to select reading texts as well as writing topics.
Continuing throughout the year	• Continue to use direct-instruction Reading and Writing Times to introduce students to new learning tasks and to add to the selection of reading responses, writing ideas, and technology assignments. • Revisit instructional groupings frequently and form new groups as needed, focusing on various reasons for grouping students: ability, specific learning needs, interests, etc.

Tracking Board

Group	First I will…	Then I will…
Group 1		
Group 2		
Group 3		
Group 4		
Group 5		

Routine Cards

PART TWO

Reading, Thinking, and Responding

A Look at Reading Time

The recess bell rings and the students enter the classroom. The teacher draws their attention to the magnetic board showing talk-partners and they quickly scan the chart for their names and sit on the carpet. Jamie is excited because Kyle is her partner; Marcus quietly sits beside David, who waves shyly; Anna whispers something in Russian to Kristina and both girls begin to giggle.

The teacher begins by setting the context for the book, asking the students to recall a time when they had really wanted something they just couldn't have. They share their ideas with their talk-partners, recalling the desired items and the reasons the students were unable to have them. After a few brief moments, the teacher introduces the Big Thinking Question. She has written the question on a chart so that students can read and think about it for the duration of the story. Today's question is, "Jeremy has to make a difficult decision. Why is it so hard for him?" After reading the question, she allows the students a moment to think about what the question is asking and paraphrases as needed.

She reads the book *Those Shoes* by Maribeth Boelts. Throughout the reading, she pauses a few times to think aloud or define an unfamiliar term. While reading, she poses a few questions and asks the students to talk to their partners. They all turn and talk, taking a minute or so to verbalize their ideas. The teacher is cautious to balance the need to pause, think, and talk with maintaining the flow of the book. She knows that pausing too frequently, or talking for too long, can interrupt the content of the book and distract students from the main message.

After reading the book, she draws the student's attention back to the Big Thinking Question. Jamie and Kyle get into a passionate dialogue; the teacher can hear them strongly stating their ideas and referring to the book to prove their answers. David and Marcus sit in silence for a few seconds and then Marcus begins to whisper his thinking to his partner. Anna and Kristina begin to talk, but the conversation quickly switches from English to Russian, as Kristina discovers that she can't find the exact words she needs to express herself in English, her new language. The teacher listens in on the various conversations, allowing sufficient time for students to fully explain their thinking.

Using a signal, the teacher indicates to the students that they should finish their conversations. They end by saying thank-you to their partners and turn to face the teacher. She repeats the Big Thinking Question. Almost every hand is raised to respond. Jamie and Kyle are practically crawling over each other, eager to share their discussion with the class. David raises a cautious hand and, when the teacher calls on him, shares his thinking with a rather coy smile. Perhaps there is time for one or two more responses. When students share simple answers, the teacher probes deeper into their thinking by asking them, "What made you think that?" or "How do you know?" Finally, Anna is asked to share. She pauses and casts a sideways glance at Kristina, who bursts into a fit of giggles once again. Anna shares Kristina's thinking, explaining that her ideas were really interesting because the story made her think of a time she had in her home country. The conversations are rich and alive. The students' ideas are profound and relevant. In this short time, the students have actively connected with a book, engaged in rich conversations, and practiced higher-order thinking.

3 Reading Around the Literacy Block

Read Aloud: Make Books Come Alive!

— *at http://lisadonohue.wordpress.com/2012/03/01/read-aloud-make-books-come-alive/*

As long as I live, I will always remember curling up in my bed and listening to my mom read my favorite childhood story, The Three Billy Goats Gruff. I recall her deepening her voice and reciting "*Who's that trip trapping across my bridge?*" and then timidly reply, "*It's just me, the littlest Billy Goat Gruff.*" Night after night, I pleaded for her to read this book to me and, night after night, she obliged.

Many years later, I remember sitting in a large lecture hall on my first day at a new university, staring wide-eyed as I listened to my professor read a story aloud. It had been more than a decade since I'd had the experience of listening to a story. The voice of Dr. Elizabeth Thorn is forever etched in my mind: "*I went to sleep with gum in my mouth, and now there's gum in my hair…and I could tell it was going to be a terrible, horrible, no good, very bad day*" (from *Alexander and the Terrible, Horrible, No Good, Very Bad Day* by Judith Viorst). Although this was many, many years ago, this text remains with me. Often on difficult days, I find myself sighing, *Well, some days are like that…even in Australia!*

Now, as a teacher, I make it a promise to read aloud to my students every day. I am always awed by the intensity with which they listen while I read. We engage in deep and thoughtful conversations. We don't simply "read" the books…we "live" the adventure. We've laughed together, cried together, and sat riveted as mysteries have unfolded in front of us. On a daily basis, we experience grand adventures together. We travel to distant times and incredible places, we enter worlds of imagination and wonder. We explore new places, new perspectives, new realities. Even if only for a short time, our classroom is transported, filled with creativity and dreams.

Modelled Reading

Modelled reading during Reading Time allows opportunities for teachers to model effective reading. Students are able to see what good readers do when they read. When we read aloud, we provide students the opportunity to learn a great deal about the reading process. We are able to explicitly teach reading and thinking strategies, promote higher-order thinking, and encourage rich conversations about texts. We are also able to teach things implicitly—things like passion for reading; reading with fluency and expression, excitement, or anticipation; and getting humor or pure enjoyment from texts. We can help foster curiosity, we can build vocabulary, we can extend beyond texts by continuing the conversation or exploring new ideas. Through this modelling, we are able to demystify the thinking processes that happen when we read. We can think out loud for students to gain an understanding of the invisible thought processes that are happening when we are reading. Modelled reading instruction is the time when we help students see the value of reading, understand the purpose of reading, and develop a passion for reading. We can use this precious time to model reading strategies and different ways of responding to reading.

Modelled reading is the vehicle through which we are able to directly teach the whole class and develop shared understanding around specific learning goals. This instructional time is far more than a half hour of entertaining children by reading a book to them. It has significant value.

Carefully selecting texts, modelling explicitly, and intentionally planning opportunities for students to think and share their ideas are keys to making a read-aloud an integral component of daily literacy instruction. By thinking aloud while reading, the teacher is able to model the complex processes that happen internally while reading a book. Students can gain an insight into the way a proficient reader reflects, questions, and engages with a text. It is this interaction between the reader and the text that forms the basis for comprehension. In order to understand a text, proficient readers engage in an ongoing dialogue with it, pausing to think and actively interpret the information they have read. This process of thinking while reading has come to the forefront in the last decade and is seen as an integral component of teaching reading comprehension. When they receive explicit, direct instruction of various reading strategies, students are able to develop a toolkit of strategies with which they can effectively interact with different texts.

Does Whole-Class Mean Undifferentiated?

As teachers, we need to differentiate our instruction in order to suit the needs of all learners in the class. If all instruction was presented in a whole-class fashion, where all students are introduced to a concept and then complete the same task, then one could argue that there is little differentiation. However, using whole-class instruction as an integral component in the gradual release of responsibility allows students to gain a shared understanding of the new skills that are being actively introduced. Differentiated instruction means that each student's strengths and needs are taken into consideration when the teacher is planning learning experiences, to ensure that each child is challenged and supported in that learning. When planning whole-class learning experiences, the teacher can take into account different students' learning styles and interests, and various strengths and needs.

While most differentiation will happen through small-group instruction, the following elements can apply to all areas of literacy instruction:

- Teachers need to set high expectations for all students, intentionally capitalizing on their strengths rather than focusing on their weaknesses.

For more on differentiated learning, see *Literacy for Learning* (Ontario Ministry of Education, 2004).

- Teachers need to use assessment as a tool to guide instruction. Teachers should use all assessment (before, during, and after) to guide instruction and provide ongoing specific feedback.
- Students should be actively engaged in inquiry in order to explore important concepts and ideas.
- Tasks need to have various points of entry and multiple forms of responding to allow students to effectively demonstrate their learning.
- Teachers need to use a variety of instructional approaches to explicitly teach various literacy skills.
- Instructional groupings need to be flexible and responsive, changing frequently in order to meet the changing needs and interests of the students. Students can work independently, with a partner, in small groups, or in a whole-class context.
- Teachers should use a range of literacy resources that vary in levels of difficulty and complexity in order to target students' different reading levels.

See page 42 for more on reading strategies.

Reading strategies can be woven throughout the literacy block in order to provide students with opportunities to learn through modelled, guided, and independent experiences. Use the Reading Time allotted to the beginning of the literacy block for direct instruction in reading when introducing students to a new reading comprehension strategy. During this time, you can begin by helping the students define the strategy and model how they would use it when reading aloud. Carefully chosen texts and intentionally selected sections are important in allowing students to see the reading strategy in action. While modelling, you might choose a few places in the text to pause and have students share their thinking out loud, so that they begin to understand the ways in which a strategy can help when interpreting a text. For example:

> *This section really helped me visualize what is happening in the book. Listen to the way the author described the things that we can see and smell in this particular scene.*

You can then choose another section of the text and invite students to share the ways in which the reading strategy helped them to better understand the text. Encouraging students to engage in conversations with each other allows them to become active participants in the reading process by sharing their thinking and by learning from the ideas of their peers.

When you extend the learning into the guided reading, students are then provided the opportunity to practice a new reading comprehension strategy in a supported setting. With the guidance of the teacher and in collaboration with their peers, students can apply the reading strategy to a text. While guided reading lessons can have many different instructional focuses—including decoding, fluency, and comprehension—they are a perfect time to ensure that students are using reading comprehension strategies in effective ways. In this way, students are able to begin to transfer their learning from the modelled reading time with the support of a guided reading text. You can reinforce the students' learning, as well as provide support when needed. By assigning a reading response, you are able to ensure that students are accurately interpreting the text and applying the reading strategy.

Finally, the students can continue their learning by applying the new reading strategy to their self-selected independent-reading books. When you provide time for students to read books of their choosing and to practice their learning in authentic ways you allow them to immediately transfer their skills.

By strategically using the various sections of the literacy block, it becomes possible to seamlessly integrate the gradual release of responsibility when introducing students to new reading comprehension strategies. The 100 Minutes framework naturally lends itself to provide daily opportunities for modelled, guided, and independent learning times. As teachers use the modelled reading time as a way of reinforcing students' learning, they are able to revisit various reading strategies as necessary. Obviously, it goes without saying that it would take more than one lesson and therefore one day to adequately teach students a new reading strategy. Flexibility remains the essential element in maintaining a true balance in literacy instruction. Teachers should consider the individual needs of their class when determining how many lessons are needed when targeting reading comprehension strategies.

Reading Strategies

"Comprehension means that readers think not only about what they are reading but what they are understanding. When readers construct meaning, they are building their store of knowledge. But along with knowledge must come understanding." —Harvey and Goudvis (2000)

Metacognition, or thinking about thinking, has become an important element in teaching reading comprehension. Over the past decade much of the work surrounding reading comprehension has focused on explicitly teaching students strategies to help them better understand the things that they read. In the book *Strategies That Work* (2000/2007), Harvey and Goudvis share their approach to teaching reading-comprehension strategies: strategies that include connecting, inferring, questioning, visualizing, determining importance, and synthesizing. These strategies have helped form effective reading-comprehension instruction. Explicit instruction in comprehension strategies helps readers better understand the things they read.

Research has shown that students who are explicitly taught a variety of reading strategies have stronger comprehension than students who are not. A study from the Netherlands (Houtveen and van de Grift, 2007) compared two groups of ten-year-old students. They found that students who were explicitly taught metacognitive reading strategies and maximized the time spent in reading instruction made significant gains and maintained these gains the following academic year; in comparison, their counterparts who received no such explicit instruction showed no such gains.

The purpose of teaching students different reading strategies is not to make them able to perform a checklist of strategies on demand, but rather so that they have a toolkit of comprehension strategies at their command with which to interpret text.

As thoughtful readers, we need to help students learn how to become aware of their inner conversations as they are reading. They need to stop, think and react to the text in ways that allow them to gain a deeper understanding of the material. Students who are actively engaged in the process of reading are continuously checking their understanding of the text. They are aware of the words they are reading, conscious of the meaning of the text. They are constructing images in their mind's eye, making sense of the actions of characters, interpreting the voice of the author, engaging in a dialogue with the text through asking questions and seeking answers, identifying the main ideas, and using details to form conclusions. A good reader keeps a running script in his or her mind, noting important and relevant details, constructing meaning from the words, and checking to make sure that it all makes sense.

The reading strategies form an essential toolkit that students can use to engage with the texts that they read. The strategies are not the goal, but the means through which we achieve the goal. The purpose of teaching students different reading strategies is not so that they can perform a checklist of strategies on demand, but rather that they have a toolkit of comprehension strategies at their command with which to interpret text. We need to help students build a repertoire of reading strategies they can apply in appropriate ways to support their comprehension when reading. By introducing students to the different comprehension strategies, we are able to explicitly model the thinking processes that help readers to develop their understanding of texts.

Why Teach Reading Strategies?

A study by Dr. Gary Woolley (2007) found that students who were struggling with comprehension were able to strengthen their mental imagery, and hence improve their comprehension through rich questioning and discussion of the text. He found that using a "personalized responsive relationship-based" approach to reading, in combination with interesting texts and student choice, resulted in students developing more-effective higher-order comprehension skills.

Defining Reading Strategies

See *Strategies That Work* (Harvey & Goudvis, 2000/2007) for more on reading strategies.

Monitoring Understanding: The purpose of reading is to make meaning from text. Readers need to constantly check to ensure that they understand the things they are reading. They may need to pause to think, reread, or self-correct something they have initially read inaccurately that has affected the meaning of the text. Good readers continuously monitor their understanding and repair their comprehension when necessary.

Visualizing: The ability to create visual images when reading is strongly linked to reading comprehension. Readers need to use all their senses to imagine the text. They may imagine the tone of a character's voice, the smell of a musty basement, or the taste of a delicious recipe. By using all their senses, readers are able to create rich mental images that assist them in imagining the text, hence strengthening their comprehension.

Determining Importance: Readers need to navigate the complexity of a text and separate the important information from the irrelevant details. They need to decide what is important to remember in order to best interpret the text as a whole. By focusing on the "big picture" of a text, readers are able to determine the main idea, the theme, or the most important information. By identifying the important information in texts, students begin to determine not only *what* is important, but also *why* it is important, and become able to provide evidence to rationalize their thinking.

Questioning: Effective readers are active participants in an intricate dialogue with the text. They ask questions and search for answers in a conversation with the author. Our personal experiences, preferences, or interests cause us to engage with the text in different ways, creating a unique interaction for each reader. Students might have questions about the actions of a character, the cause of a conflict, a specific element in a book, or an element that they found particularly puzzling when reading.

Connecting: When we read, we find ways the text connects to our prior experiences, our existing knowledge, our own lives, other books we have read, or things we know about the world. The background knowledge that we bring to a text helps us to relate to and interpret the subject matter. When we connect to texts, they become personally relevant. Through our connections, we can relate to the actions of a character, understand the historical context or setting of a story, or analyze new information based on our prior experiences or knowledge.

Inferring: When readers make inferences, they make assumptions about what is implied, but not stated, in the text. They go beyond what is literally written and make thoughtful conclusions using clues from the text. By combining their own thinking with the information provided in the text, readers are able to determine the theme or moral of a story, identify the feelings of a character, and generally "read between the lines" of a text.

Synthesizing: By combining our existing knowledge with new information as we read, we often have "ah-ha!" moments when we form new ideas, opinions, or interpretations. As a reader integrates new information, makes judgments and conclusions, or combines information from different sources, that reader is synthesizing the text by creating something new. By merging our thinking with the author's, we are able to respond in a way that is based both on the text and our personal experiences and existing knowledge.

HOT and Critical Literacy

As students begin to think more deeply about texts, they need to rely on higher-order thinking. This approach to thinking about texts encourages students to question, explore, and reflect on their reading. When students engage in HOT (Higher-Order Thinking), they are able to explore plausible answers to questions and defend their ideas with evidence or proof. They can synthesize information from a variety of sources, including their personal experiences, in order to justify their opinion or answer.

In today's world, students are constantly being bombarded with different media messages and texts. They need to develop skills to navigate through this wide array of information. Developing critical-literacy skills helps students begin to think more deeply about the texts they encounter as well as the texts they create. As a critically literate reader, one is able to read beyond the literal message and think deeply about the text. When we teach students to be critically literate, they understand that texts are written by others and may contain elements of the author's bias. They examine texts in order to understand the author's purpose or intent, to access the underlying messages behind given works, or even to think about whose voices are being represented or silenced. They are given permission to question the authority of texts, and realize that texts reflect the author's beliefs, choices, or positions.

Critical literacy is not a subject; neither is it an element of literacy that stands on its own. It is a lens through which students can learn to view all texts. It should become an integrated component of classroom discussions, an ongoing catalyst for conversations, and a way that students begin to think and react to different texts.

Talking About Texts

Students should be given frequent opportunities to talk about texts. When students engage in talk, they are processing and integrating their learning in meaningful ways. According to Fountas and Pinnell (2001), "We talk with each other to sort out what we don't understand, to get more information, to gather different perspectives or to express emotions. Talk expands our understanding and helps us clarify our own feelings; it is a tool for learning."

However, it is not sufficient to provide time to talk. In order for talk to be truly beneficial, it needs to be focused and robust. Students need time to talk about things that are relevant, engaging, challenging, and authentic. We want to fill our learning time with bursts of thoughtful conversations that help propel the learning forward. We need to provide opportunities to talk, give students rich questions and topics to talk about, and create a community where talking-to-learn is the norm.

Talk-to-Learn

Accountable talk is a valuable classroom strategy that encourages students to engage in rich conversations with each other. Janet Allen (2002) suggests that accountable talk can promote cognitive collaboration and active learning; it should be meaningful, respectful, and beneficial to the speaker and the listener. When students communicate, they learn how to articulate their thinking, justify their ideas, and question the opinions of others. Talk can be a powerful vehicle through which students can explore higher-order thinking and inquire collaboratively. Students can communicate, collaborate, question, and explore ideas. When given frequent opportunities for active communication, students develop confidence, are encouraged to take risks, and ultimately learn to express their thinking in complete and sophisticated ways.

Learning is a social process; intentionally orchestrated opportunities to talk allow students to extend their own thinking and the ideas of others. When working as a whole class, students can engage in frequent talk-times in order to ensure they are actively participating in the learning process. Students use accountable talk as a way of strengthening their understanding through collaboration with others. They can challenge another's opinion or idea through questioning, or justify their thinking by providing evidence for their ideas. Through talk, students can explore their own ideas more fully as well as build on the ideas of others. Students should feel comfortable sharing opinions and personal perspectives. Accountable talk can be a valuable tool during all areas of literacy instruction, from whole-class instruction to small-group guided sessions. Through ongoing collaboration and purposeful talk-times, students learn how to appreciate differing opinions, disagree respectfully, build on the ideas of others, and integrate new information in order to enhance their understanding.

According to Shirley Brice Heath, talk is not only beneficial, but also essential for certain literacy skills to develop: "For those groups of individuals who do not have occasions to talk about what and how meanings are achieved in written materials, important cognitive and interpretive skills, which are basic to being literate, do not develop" (in Daniels, 1994).

When we think of talk in relation to reading, we realize the need to provide students with opportunities to engage in conversations about texts in a variety of settings. This should include talk-times during direct instruction, small-group conversations during guided reading, and opportunities to share their thoughts about their reading informally with their peers. Opportunities for talk should be woven throughout the literacy block, fostering a community where students value and respect each other's thoughts, ideas, and opinions.

Gambrell and Amalasi (1996) believe that student discussions bring together the skills of listening, speaking, and thinking, since participants exchange ideas as they respond and react to the text and the ideas of others. They feel that meaningful classroom discussions enable readers to enhance the meaning that is generated from a text:

> Although individual readers can construct their own interpretation of literary works, interpretive work within a group is more powerful. In a group, readers share their own understandings and significant insights and must convince others of the value of their insights. This type of negotiation involves the exchange of ideas in which readers present support for their positions and consider the arguments of others in presenting counter positions. Such activities reflect problem solving and reasoning and produce discoveries about literature that no one reader by him or herself could likely construct alone.

Developing a Talk-Centred Classroom

When creating a classroom in which students talk-to-learn, it is important to develop a sense of community and mutual respect. Taking time to establish the norms for talk-times is a valuable investment at the beginning of the year. Working with students, you can use modelling and direct instruction to help students begin to understand what effective talk-time would look like. They need to understand the role they will play when given opportunities to talk. This might take the form of structured talk opportunities (such as accountable-talk partners during Reading Time), small-group chats during guided-learning times, or informal partnering during other collaborative learning opportunities. Regardless of when the talk happens or what the talk is about, students need to develop positive habits in order to ensure that they are getting the most out of their talk-time.

The creation of success criteria for talk-partners can help guide students when they engage in conversations. Students might find it helpful to role-play the different elements in the success criteria, or even act out Yes and No examples. In one classroom, students posed for pictures showing each target behavior as both a Yes image and a No image; for example, "We sit close together and use a quiet voice" was illustrated with (a) *Yes!* (an image of students sitting side by side) and (b) *No!* (an image of the same students reaching across a table with "loud" expressions, appearing to be shouting). These were displayed on a bulletin board and served as a visual reminder for students about how to use their talk-times effectively. Not only were these fun to create but they also helped to reinforce the important aspects of how students should use talk to learn.

Maximizing Comprehension through Talk

Talk is a powerful tool for enabling students to engage with texts, think deeply about different ideas, consider varying perspectives, and provide evidence to justify their thinking or prove their point. When reading aloud to students during Reading Time, intentionally weave in opportunities for students to talk with each other about the text. This can be done in a number of ways:

1. During direct-instruction times, when reading aloud to students, pause occasionally to share your thinking or pose a question to the class. Typically, when you pose a question to the class, the students raise their hands to respond. But what would happen if, when you asked a question, all students were invited to share their answers? Chaos? Not necessarily. If students are able to share their thinking with a partner, then they can all have an opportunity to be heard. In a simple strategy called Think–Pair–Share, students are given the opportunity to all respond to questions posed by the teacher. This approach for incorporating talk into instructional times allows for all students to have their voices heard. Simply stated, when reading a text aloud, the teacher pauses to ask a question to the students: a simple question, such as "What do you predict will happen next?"; a question that focuses on a specific reading strategy, such as "What clues tell you how the main character is feeling right now?"; or a more complex question, such as "What is the lesson the author wants us to learn from this text?" When provided with two to three opportunities to pause, think, and respond during the reading of a text, students are able to interact with the text, share their thinking, and collaborate with their peers.

Think–Pair–Share

After posing a question:
1. Teacher allows sufficient time for students to think independently about their response.
2. Students turn to a partner and take turns sharing their thinking.
3. Some students might choose to share their ideas with the class as a whole.

2. When introducing students to a text for a read-aloud lesson, consider framing it with a Big Thinking Question (BTQ). This can be a question posed at the beginning of reading that can be revisited during or after the reading. Posing a question that requires students to reflect on the text as a whole or justify their opinion will help generate more meaningful conversations than posing questions that can be answered with information explicitly stated in the text. By introducing texts with a BTQ, the teacher encourages students to think critically about the information they are encountering during the reading. Revisiting the BTQ provides students an opportunity to talk with their partners, sharing their thinking and responding to the ideas of others. Using BTQs and talk-time during direct-instruction times in reading allows stu-

dents to think deeply about texts and respond orally. This increases student engagement by having them become active participants in the lesson. BTQs and talk-time can be used to target any reading skill, ranging from reading comprehension strategies to HOT questions and critical literacy. Students are able to immediately actively engage with the text and with each other in meaningful discussions; they are able to express their ideas and challenge the ideas of others; they can provide evidence to prove their thinking or share personal knowledge that helps justify their responses. By intentionally incorporating talk-times, teachers are able to monitor students' thinking and learning. These brief yet powerful opportunities for talk are critical in helping students become robust thinkers.

SAMPLE QUESTIONS

Instead of asking…	Try asking…
• Why did the main character cheat on his test?	• Do you think it is ever okay to cheat on a test?
• How did the main character feel at the end of the book?	• How do you know that the main character learned an important lesson through the book?
• What happened when the main character was caught?	• Do you think justice was served when the main character was caught?
• What happened when he broke the rules?	• Is it ever okay to break the rules?
• How did the main character solve the problem?	• What obstacle do you think was the hardest for the main character to overcome?
• Which character was your favorite?	• If you were the main character, how might you have tried to solve the problem?
• Where does the text take place?	• Do you agree with the decisions made by the main character?
• How old do you think the main character is?	• What are some of the traits you admire most about the main character in the story?
	• Who do you think was the hero of the story? Why do you think that?
	• Do you think the main character was treated fairly?
	• If this was a real person, would you choose him/her as a friend? Why or why not?
	• What is the most important lesson that the author wants us to learn from the book? How do you know that?
	• What audience did the author have in mind when he/she wrote this book?
	• What facts do you think are the most important to remember from this text? Why?
	• How do you know if this text is fact or fiction?

Accountable Talk Partners

As a way of increasing accountability, consider intentionally partnering students together as talk-partners. By strategically partnering students, you can ensure that all students have an equal opportunity to share and be heard. With intentional talk-partners, you can maximize learning opportunities for all students by strategically separating students when necessary, allowing students to work with a greater variety of peers, and creating thoughtful partnerships in which both partners will benefit.

You might place each student's name on a small card with a magnet on the back. These cards can be displayed on the board in a list, helping students to identify their talk-partner. This allows students to sit beside their talk-partners during lessons in order to easily turn and talk. Talk-partners should be changed frequently (on a daily or weekly basis) in order to maximize the level of accountability during partner conversations.

As opportunities for talk are woven throughout the literacy block, students can join in thoughtful conversations during direct instruction, guided reading, and collaborative learning. In a community where students use talk as a vehicle for learning, they will have greater opportunities for actively engaging with texts and building on the ideas of others.

What Is Text?

What students are reading is as important as *how* students are reading. The term *text* can refer to a wide variety of print and online media. Our classrooms need to reflect the multimedia environment in which we all live. Messages shared in the media often include complex combinations of words, images, and sounds. If you increase students' experiences to include multiple forms of text, students will gain a better understanding of how to interact with the world through the texts they encounter. Many students are able to identify the differences between fiction and nonfiction texts; however, there are multiple forms of media texts that challenge readers to think critically about the information. Students need to analyze, evaluate, and interpret messages they encounter through various forms of communication. When students are critically literate, they begin to analyze the messages they encounter, asking questions such as *Who created the message? Who was the intended audience of the message? Is the message biased in any ways? Whose message is being shared? Whose voice is being silenced? What strategies did the author use to engage the audience?* When we include media texts, we encourage students to consider messages from different perspectives and to think critically about the form, content, and meaning.

How can we seamlessly integrate media literacy into our instruction? By including rich media texts as options for read-alouds during Reading Time, we can model ways of thinking about these different texts as we interact with them. Weaving a variety of texts into guided-reading instruction and independent reading also provides the time that students need to apply and practice taking their own critical stance with different texts. During guided-reading sessions consider using a media text (such as a news website, a video, a poster, a commercial, or even graphic text) as a way of framing discussions about these texts. Analysis of media could continue into independent reading time and include resources like newspapers, magazines, or links to online resources. During AWARD Time, technology activities could include accessing and responding to specific sites or creating media works as a response to reading, writing, or cross-curricular connections.

Unprepared access to the Internet can be overwhelming and potentially disastrous for youngsters. It is highly recommended that teachers take the time to preview sites and then bookmark or compile them for easy access on a class website or Moodle.

For example, National Geographic for Kids has a wide variety of Animal Creature Feature pages. These pages are filled with text, videos, maps, and other interactive elements. This site could be used during modelled reading, guided reading, or independent reading. It could be combined with reading response through the use of thoughtfully posed questions. Students might be provided with a number of animals from which they choose, selecting a few that they would like to read and respond to. In this way, students are able to self-select texts from a virtual library.

Reproduced with permission from National Geographic Kids

Possible Reading-Response Question: Dolphins are considered among the most intelligent creatures. Why do you think this is true? Use evidence from the text and your own ideas to explain your thinking.

The chart on page 51 includes some of the animals featured on the National Geographic for Kids website and samples of questions you could use to create reading responses for students.

Brachychampsa Montana	Why do you think this prehistoric creature has adapted and survived when many other animals did not?
Anaconda	An anaconda is a dangerous predator. Explain the features that allow it to be such a powerful creature.
Chimpanzee	Chimpanzees sometimes act like humans. Give some examples of their behavior that would be similar to a human.
Giant Panda	Giant pandas are endangered. How do you think their diet and the presence of humans have affected the panda population?
Emperor Penguin	The emperor penguin is the only creature that stays on the Antarctic's open ice throughout the harsh winter. Explain why it stays and how it survives.
American Bullfrog	If you saw a frog in a pond, how would you know whether or not it was an American bullfrog?

Another valuable site that can help incorporate media texts into daily literacy experiences is Teaching Kids News (www.teachkidsnews.com). This site contains articles about current world news in a child-friendly format. The content is updated daily and is accessible and suitable for children; the news articles are short and engaging for readers from Grades 2 to 8. Teaching Kids News follows through on its promise to provide "timely, relevant news articles for kids, educators in the classroom and parents at home." In addition to the articles, Teaching Kids News also includes various writing prompts and reading questions to accompany each article—a simple yet brilliant way of incorporating media texts into reading and writing. Students can peruse the site, select a news article that they feel is interesting or important, and then respond to it.

Screenshot reproduced with permission from Teaching Kids News, www.teachkidsnews.com

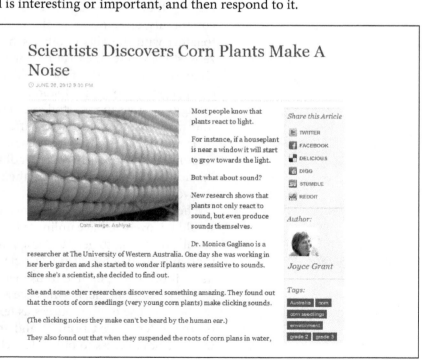

Using Social Media to Connect

Tweeting with one of my student's favorite authors, I was able to remove the classroom walls and help that student connect with the author behind the words.

Many children's authors use social media as a way of connecting with their audience and providing a way for readers to share their thoughts and questions with them. While you might not find it possible or practical to have a classroom filled with seven-year-old Tweeps, consider starting a class Twitter account. If students wish to connect with or follow specific authors, these writers are generally quite easy to find, either through Twitter or their own websites. Most authors have a Contact Me section on their websites. Since this would require an e-mail address in order to receive a response, consider creating a class e-mail account strictly for this purpose. Young readers are often awestruck when they realize that authors are real, live people who they can connect with through social media.

Tweets shared with permission from Marina Cohen, @marinacohen

Lisa Donohue @Lisa_Donohue   26 Apr
@marinacohen ...my fav quote from an 9 yr old: I like Marina Cohen's books b/c the characters are interesting & the author is sophisticated.
Expand

marina cohen @marinacohen   26 Apr
@Lisa_Donohue wow. Not sure I've been called that before. I like it! Though I'd say that 9yr old is the sophisticated one!!
Hide conversation   Reply   Retweet   Favorite

We're Talking Digital

Talk can take many forms. Students can engage in rich conversations face-to-face. Or they can use digital tools to connect with people outside their school or community, an option that allows them to talk first-hand with experts or learn together with students in other schools, cities, or even countries. As global citizens, students are able to engage in world events and actively communicate with children in other parts of the world. Digital tools can be used in all aspects of a literacy program to support students' reading, writing, and communication skills. Using online resources, students can read about current world events, research information, and engage with different forms of media to strengthen and apply their reading skills. They can also create and share a variety of media works in response to the things they are reading. When digital tools are integrated into the literacy block, students can use their time to read, create, share, and respond to the work of others.

The reality of budget restrictions is a challenge that all teachers face. While it would be lovely to have unlimited access to digital tools, it is most likely that we are all struggling to get our hands on these tools. But when we consider digital tools and media literacy as a vehicle for delivering content, rather than a subject itself, it becomes possible to use whatever tools are available in the most effective way. For example, having access to one computer and an LCD projector, the teacher can use online sources as text during direct-instruction times, focusing on the different text features and strengthening students' media awareness. If teachers have access to only a few classroom computers or devices, they can be used during guided-reading times, possibly to provide the text for discussion. With access to as few as five computers or devices, teachers can create a designated section of AWARD Time in which students work independently using these tools. Teachers can bookmark sites that students need to visit, download apps that support specific skill development, or provide assignments that require students to create and share media works. There is really no need for a class set of devices or computers. By integrating media awareness and digital literacy into the 100 Minutes framework (through direct instruction, guided groups, and independent work times), teachers allow students to use the resources available to them in the most effective and efficient manner. As we work our way through the realities and challenges, we need to be flexible and creative to maximize the resources we have available to our students.

4

Reading Response

As you build the literacy block (see Chapter 2), students develop an understanding that there are times when they may be learning by completing a range of tasks. For example, one group of students might be working on independent reading while another group is working on guided reading, or some students might be having a writing conference while others are writing independently. We begin by introducing students to reading responses during the Reading Time of the literacy block. Through the vehicles of direct instruction and guided reading, students begin to see how they can use their reading response as a way of reflecting and sharing their thinking about the texts they are reading. At first, you might find it beneficial to introduce students to only a limited number of reading response formats, so that they can develop an understanding of the requirements of each task and the way it will work in their literacy routines. As time progresses, it is important to constantly revisit the tasks that students are using, in order to ensure that they are responding to their texts and increase the complexity and selections of tasks that students can complete.

Reading response can provide a much-needed element of accountability to students' independent reading time. It allows the teacher a greater insight into the students' thinking about their reading, as well as a means of monitoring the ways in which they are applying the skills they are learning. The sequence with which students rotate through the tasks during AWARD Time will make the difference between busy-work and intentionally applying and practicing the skills they are learning. When reading response immediately follows guided reading, students are able to respond to the guided-reading text as a way of recording and demonstrating their understanding. This creates an intentional sequence of tasks: the teacher is able to actively teach students a skill through guided reading and then students are immediately able to practice it on their own. Following a similar logic, the next day the same group of students could begin to transfer their new learning by reading independently and then completing a reading response for the text they have chosen on their own. Following the framework provided through the gradual release of responsibility, the sequence of learning starts with direct instruction (possibly through whole-class instruction), supported through guided reading (small-group instruction), followed by guided practice, and finally application of learning to reading through independent reading time.

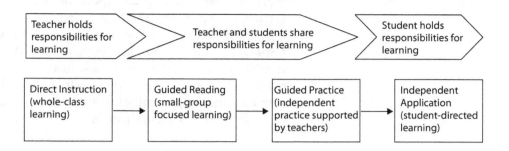

Framing Guided Practice and Independent Application

One of the biggest challenges we face as teachers is assessment of independent reading. When students are reading independently, we can observe the way they interact with texts, whether they stick with various books or frequently abandon them. We can observe whether or not they seem engaged with the books they are reading by whether or not they are actively reading them. We can observe their body language and make informed conclusions about their reading habits. However, the internal processes that students use when reading—the thinking part of reading—is more difficult for us to access. How do we know what students are thinking as readers? How can we ensure that the strategies we have been actively teaching them are actually being transferred to their independent reading? Is there a way that we can monitor their thinking when they are reading on their own? While guided reading sessions and conversations we have with students about their reading provide some insight into their thinking, there remains the challenge of monitoring students' thinking and the transfer of their learning to their independent reading. How can we guide their learning when they are all reading different books? Is it possible to ensure that students are actively practicing the skills they are learning through other aspects of the literacy time? And is there a way that we can monitor and assess this in order to further drive instruction and guide students' learning?

The most effective way of monitoring students' independent reading is through the use of reading responses. Through a range of reading-response tasks, students can be encouraged to reflect on their reading and share their thinking in a way that can be easily monitored. There have been many different models for creating reading responses, including reading-response journals, writing letters between students and teachers, and other variations. Over the years, I have found that the most effective way of encouraging students to reflect on their reading has come from using a range of different tools, prompts, and response modes. When students respond to reading using the same format, initially they are excited to embrace the new approach; however, as the year goes on the routine becomes stale. While the element of reading response remains essential throughout the year, teachers should consider embedding elements of choice and using a range of tools through which students may respond. For example, students can select from a range of Response Cards (see pages 61–68) to create a written response or they might use digital tools as a way of reflecting their reading through different media. In this way, throughout the year students will experience a variety of ways to share their thinking about the texts they are reading.

See pages 61–68 for reading-response task cards. For a wider selection of reading-response tasks, you might check out *Independent Reading Inside the Box* (Donohue, 2008).

Regardless of the form the reading response takes, it provides students with the much-needed time to practice, consolidate, and apply the skills that have been actively taught during the instructional portions of the literacy block. Allowing students to choose their own texts and the way in which they would like to respond to them ensures differentiation for all students based on their interests, as well as on strengths and needs. Reading response provides students with a purpose for their new learning and strengthens their skills. Finally, it provides us with countless opportunities to assess students' learning and thinking and, with this information, we can shape our instruction more purposefully.

Introducing Reading Response during Reading Time

(Instructional time: approximately 25 minutes)
Begin by gathering the students on the carpet or as a large group at their desks.

> *We have been working really hard to develop our reading and writing skills. We have had opportunities to read independently, and we have all had a turn to read with the teacher. But, as I was watching you read, I started to wonder what you were thinking while you were reading. Can you think for a moment about some of the things you think about when you are reading?*

Allow students a few moments to think about this question, then encourage them to share their ideas with a partner. Depending on students' age and previous reading experiences, their responses will vary greatly. Share with students some of the things that you think about when you are reading. For example, you might say, "When I'm reading a very exciting book, I feel like I'm watching a movie in my head. I can imagine the characters and sometimes I even think that I know what their voices sound like."

> *When I am thinking really hard, it is impossible for you to see the work that I am doing in my head. And when you are thinking really hard, it is impossible for me to see the work that you are doing in your head. That is why we are going to use reading responses as a way for you to share the thinking that you are doing when you are reading. Why do you think it is important that you can share your thinking with me?*

Allow students to share their ideas with their partners. After students have had an opportunity to talk with a partner, select a few students to share their ideas with the whole class.

> *There are many different ways that we can share our thinking about our reading. What are some of the ways that we can respond to reading?*

Again, allow students time to reflect and share their ideas. As they share, record their thinking on chart paper or the interactive whiteboard to keep for later reference.

Why are reading responses important?	What are some ways that we can respond to reading?
• *We can share the thinking that is happening in our heads* • *The teacher can make sure we are understanding the things that we are reading* • *We can practice the things we are learning with our own books*	• *Drawing pictures* • *Writing about our thinking* • *Talking about our thinking*

Today, I am going to show you one way that you might share your thinking.

Model a reading-response task. Begin by sharing the task with students and ask them to keep it in mind as you read a text. Read a text aloud to the students, pausing to reflect, share your thinking, and pose questions for the students to think and talk about. After reading, model how you might complete the reading response task. If possible, use a document camera so that you can write directly on the task template, or use large chart paper so that it is easy for all students to see the sample. You might wish to explicitly draw their attention to important elements in your response (e.g., providing evidence from the text, giving examples, drawing on prior experiences, making connections, etc).

> *You can see that this reading response helps you see the things that I am thinking when I am reading. The next time we meet for guided reading, we are going to do a reading response together. We are going to use the text that we read for guided reading, and then we can use a reading response to show our thinking.*

Depending on the age and ability of the students, you might model reading responses a number of times before beginning to introduce the reading-response tasks through guided reading. Younger learners might benefit from seeing the same (or similar) reading response modelled repeatedly with different texts, whereas older students would be more likely to respond to the modelling of a greater variety of reading responses. As always, it is important to consider each group of learners when establishing and developing elements of the literacy block.

Moving Beyond Day One

As students become more comfortable with the requirements of reading responses through modelling and guided reading, they will be better able to transfer these skills to their independent-reading texts. At first, it is beneficial for students to be introduced to a reading-response task through direct instruction or guided reading. This allows students time to think and collaborate on ways in which they can respond. For example, during guided reading, students might be presented with the reading response task of visualizing a character. Students could use a shared text to think, talk, and respond to this particular reading response. On the following day, the students then continue to extend and apply their learning by completing the same reading-response task in relation to their own independent reading text; thereby, they use their ability to visualize a character from a book that they have selected themselves.

Once students are comfortable with this routine, it becomes possible to focus more on a particular reading skill or strategy (e.g., making inferences), and then present students with a selection of reading responses to choose from in order to respond to their independent-reading texts. In this way, students are able to apply something that they have learned through guided instruction, and then transfer it to their own reading.

A simple classroom organizational tool you might find helpful is an interactive bulletin board with pockets on it. Each pocket can be labelled with a specific reading strategy or skill, and can contain a variety of reading responses that are specifically designed to target that strategy or skill. Students are able to self-select a reading-response task that will strength the skills they have been working on through guided reading and can begin to apply and transfer these skills through independent reading. When students meet again for guided reading, they can bring their completed reading responses as a way for you to easily monitor and assess their learning and to use this information to guide further discussions.

As students become more comfortable with this routine, a visual tracking board might help them stay organized. This will make it easy for them to see which literacy elements they are working on, and when. On a tracking board, this might look a little like this:

SAMPLE TRACKING BOARD: DAY 1

Group Name	First I will...	Then I will...
Group 1	GUIDED READING	READING RESPONSE

SAMPLE TRACKING BOARD: DAY 2

Group Name	First I will...	Then I will...
Group 1	INDEPENDENT READING	READING RESPONSE

The gradual release of responsibility is created by initially working with students directly through guided reading and then immediately following with a reading response. The following day, students apply and transfer their learning by reading independently and completing another reading response for a self-selected text. This lets them immediately transfer the skills learned through guided reading to their independent-reading texts; similarly, when the reading response is modelled or supported through guided reading, students are then able to independently transfer and apply this learning to their own independent books.

Reading-Response Tasks

Using reading responses, students can apply a variety of strategies to their independent reading. These tasks are intended to support and enhance teaching and learning. It is not intended that teachers substitute direct instruction of reading skills with worksheets, but rather that they enhance existing teaching practice with reading response in order to provide opportunities for students to practice and strengthen the skills that they have been taught.

The research clearly demonstrates that students need to be actively taught reading strategies in order to become proficient in their use. Pressley (2000) believes that instructions aimed at increasing comprehension abilities should focus on improving word-level competencies, building background knowledge, and establishing the use of comprehension strategies. These need to become a regular component in literacy instruction.

Reading-Response Journals

While the structure provided on the reading-response task cards can be helpful to some students, others might prefer to respond by writing in a reading-response journal. Teachers can provide reading-response journals in which each student can either write or glue in the task cards they have selected to complete. Teachers can copy the task card prompts and place them in pocket folders on an interactive bulletin board; this way, students can select the prompt/question to which they would like to respond. For younger students, you might find it necessary to enlarge the task cards.

When we think of reading-response journals, usually a notebook comes to mind. However, it is possible for students to create digital response journals as well. As a way of integrating technology, students can create online journals in which they respond to their independent-reading books. The journal could take the form of a blog (which can be shared publically or limited to sharing within the class) or a journal (which can be kept private and shared only between the student and the teacher). Within a digital journal, students might choose to respond in a variety of formats, including a wide range of media options. By being allowed to integrate media into reading responses, students are able to actively create a variety of forms of media for different purposes and audiences. For example, they can make a poster to promote a text, shoot a video to illustrate a portion of a book, create a movie trailer for a selected text, or even design a comic strip to show an important event in a book. In this manner, students can use their Tech Time (during AWARD Time; see page 27), as a way of integrating a wide range of skills. Tech Time should always be purposefully connected to the learning that is happening in other parts of the literacy block. Using it to create digital reading responses would be one way of maximizing students' learning; i.e., ensuring that their time is used to consolidate and extend their learning.

Some tasks can be easily adapted as digital tasks that use a variety of digital tools as a way of responding. The reading-response tasks provided can be used as a starting point: you might change or add to them in order to best cater to the individual learning needs of your specific class. The tasks can be used in a variety of ways as students respond to their reading, and might serve as a starting point for reading-response journals, regardless of which form they may take (written or digital).

The reading-response tasks that follow on pages 61–68 are divided into eight categories. You can introduce students to one set of skills at a time and then continue to build on their increasing repertoire of reading skills. Each task card can be reproduced for students to write on, or you might create master templates that students can then reproduce and place in their own reading-response notebooks.

Reading Comprehension Strategies

Visualizing: Using all our senses to create rich mental images of a text

Determining Importance: Identifying the main idea, the theme, or the most important information in a text

Questioning: Engaging in a dialogue with the text by asking questions and searching for answers

Connecting: Using prior experience, existing knowledge, and other books we have read to help interpret and understand the text

Inferring: Making thoughtful conclusions or assumptions about what is implied but not stated in the text

Synthesizing: Combining our existing knowledge with new information as we read to form something new or original

HOT: Engaging in Higher-Order Thinking to explore plausible answers and defend ideas with evidence from the text or our own experiences

For a wider selection of Reading Response tasks, see *Independent Reading Inside the Box* (Donohue, 2009).

See pages 69–70 for a chart containing questions you can use to create other reading-response tasks for reading strategies.

The reading-response tasks provide opportunities for students to practice and apply the various reading comprehension strategies (i.e., Visualizing, Determining Importance, Questioning, Connecting, Inferring, and Synthesizing). They also provide a framework for students to use HOT (Higher-Order Thinking) prompts.

The Word Skills reading-response tasks on page 61 can help students explore words and word patterns through authentic reading experiences. Readers generate word meanings and integrate them into existing vocabulary through repeated exposure in meaningful contexts. The tasks are designed to strengthen students' vocabulary and word skills. Some tasks are intended to encourage students to attend to new and interesting vocabulary, some introduce students to various parts of speech, and others help students develop an understanding of new words. Because students encounter new words in all text forms, these tasks are easily used for both fiction and nonfiction texts.

Reading-Response Task Cards: Word Skills

Word Choice

Find a passage from the text that shows how the author has used his/her choice of words to help share the message. It might be a very descriptive part of a story or a very informative section of a nonfiction resource. Which words were the most powerful to you as a reader?

_____

_____

_____

_____

_____

_____

_____

_____

Glossary

Create a glossary of new vocabulary that you've learned while reading. Beside each word write its meaning. You might need to check in a dictionary or with another source to verify that you're sure what the word means.

_____

_____

_____

_____

_____

_____

_____

_____

_____

Word Collector

Become a **word collector** of interesting and unique words. Keep a record of words that you discover that you think are worth collecting. Put a star beside the ones that you think you could use yourself.

MY WORD COLLECTION

Draw it!

Choose six words that were really interesting, important, or new to you. Create a picture to help you remember what each word means. Beside each word, record the page that you found it on, so that you can explain these words to a friend.

Pembroke Publishers © 2012 *100 Minutes* by Lisa Donohue ISBN 978-1-55138-276-0

Reading-Response Task Cards: Visualizing

VISUALIZING

1000 Words in a Picture!
Some people say that a picture is worth a thousand words. Create a picture or a diagram that will represent one of the most important ideas in your text. Add as many details as possible.

VISUALIZING

5 Senses
Choose a really descriptive passage from your text. Try to describe it using as many senses as possible.

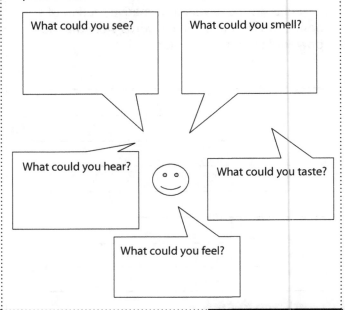

What could you see?

What could you smell?

What could you hear?

What could you taste?

What could you feel?

VISUALIZING

Words Have Power!
Select a part of the text that you were able to visualize clearly. Draw an image to share your thinking. Include evidence from the text that supports your picture.
The text said

_____

_____

_____

_____

In my mind I imagined

VISUALIZING

Sense This!
Although we have five senses, we sometimes use one of them more than the others. Describe how you used one of your senses to help you better understand the text. Give examples from the text to support your thinking.

_____

_____

_____

_____

_____

_____

_____

_____

_____

Pembroke Publishers © 2012 *100 Minutes* by Lisa Donohue ISBN 978-1-55138-276-0

Reading-Response Task Cards: Determining Importance

What's The BIG Idea?

What do you think is the main idea in the text? Use evidence from the text and your own ideas to support your thinking.

_____

_____

_____

_____

_____

_____

_____

_____

_____

What's Most Important?

Choose three important ideas from the text. Put them in order from the most important to the least important. Explain why you thought each idea belonged where you put it.

	Ideas from the Text	Rationale
Least Important Idea ↑ ↓ Most Important Idea		

Sequencing Ideas

Summarize three of the most important ideas from the text. Use sequencing words to show the order in which the events occurred.

Interesting vs. Important

Describe three ideas from the text that stood out in your mind. Tell whether each one was interesting, important, or both.

1 _____

_____

_____

2 _____

_____

_____

3 _____

_____

_____

Reading-Response Task Cards: Questioning

Ask the Author

If you could ask the author anything about the text what would you want to know? Write a letter to the author asking him/her to answer some questions that you have about the text.

Dear _____ ,

_____

_____

_____

_____

_____

_____   Ask your teacher if you
_____   can look on the Internet to
find the author's contact
information. Wouldn't it
be fun if he/she actually
answered your questions!

Ask the Characters

Imagine you are able to meet the characters from the text. What questions would you ask them?

Character	Questions I would like to ask

Ask Yourself

What questions did you ask yourself while reading that helped you to understand the text?

_____

_____

_____

_____

_____

_____

_____

_____

_____

_____

_____

Finding the Answers

What questions did you have as you were reading the text? If you were able to find the answers, record them so you can share them with a friend.

Questions I had:	Answers I discovered:

Reading-Response Task Cards: Connecting

In My Life...

Does this text remind you of something you have personally experienced? Have you been in a similar situation, met a similar person, or been to a similar place? Describe how your experiences are similar to the text.

_____

_____

_____

_____

_____

_____

_____

_____

_____

Venn Diagram

Use a Venn Diagram to compare this text to another one that you have read on a similar topic or by the same author.

Meaningful Links

Create a chain showing how the text is connected to your personal experiences. In the first link include an important idea from the text, in the last link describe a personal experience that helped you connect to the text. In the middle, explain how your personal experience helped you understand the text better.

The Text Made Me Think

Complete the chart, showing the connections you made while reading.

Ideas I connected with	These ideas made me think of...

Reading-Response Task Cards: Inferring

Lessons Learned

What lessons can you learn from this text? How does the author teach you these lessons without directly stating them?

_____

_____

_____

_____

_____

_____

_____

_____

Author's Intent

What do you think was the author's purpose when he/she wrote this text? What was the message he/she wanted to share with you? Use information from the text to support your thinking.

_____

_____

_____

_____

_____

_____

_____

_____

Character's Thoughts!

Are there times when you can determine what characters are thinking from their words and actions? Describe one of these times. Provide evidence from the text to support your thinking.

_____

_____

_____

_____

_____

_____

_____

Big Changes

Compare the way the main character feels at the beginning of the text to the way he/she feels at the end. Use examples from the story to explain your thinking.

What happens to cause this change?

_____

_____

_____

_____

Reading-Response Task Cards: Synthesizing

SYNTHESIZING

Media Promotion

Create a media piece to promote the text. For example, you might create a poster, podcast, movie trailer, or commercial.

SYNTHESIZING

Reflective Reading

After reading this text, has your thinking changed in some way? Did you learn a lesson, change your point of view, or think about an issue from a different perspective? Explain how your thinking changed and what part of the text influenced you.

_____

_____

_____

_____

_____

_____

_____

_____

SYNTHESIZING

Changing Point of View

If you could hear this text from another point of view, whose perspective would you like to hear? Why?

_____

_____

_____

_____

_____

_____

_____

_____

_____

SYNTHESIZING

Lesson Learned

What is an important lesson you learned from this text? Explain how this might affect the way you act or think in the future.

_____

_____

_____

_____

_____

_____

_____

_____

Reading-Response Task Cards: HOT

HOT

Fairness
Do you think the main character was treated fairly? Why or why not? Give examples from the text to support your thinking.

_____

_____

_____

_____

_____

_____

_____

_____

_____

HOT

Judging Actions
Do you agree with the decisions made by the main character? Would you have acted differently? Explain your thinking.

_____

_____

_____

_____

_____

_____

_____

_____

_____

HOT

Important Issues
What issues do you think are important to the author? How does he/she share this with you? Do you agree that these issues are important? Justify your thinking.

_____

_____

_____

_____

_____

_____

_____

_____

HOT

Convincing Argument
What are three ideas that the author has convinced you are important? What evidence from the text helped to persuade you?

Create Your Own Reading-Response Tasks

Word Skills

- How many words can you find to use instead of the word "said"?
- Find three words that are new or interesting. Use a dictionary to find the definition, a synonym, and an antonym.
- Create a glossary for your text.
- Create a picture dictionary for your text: record new and interesting words, and then draw pictures to illustrate their meanings.
- Make a chart showing different nouns, verbs, adjectives, and adverbs you discover while reading.

Visualizing

- Write a brief paragraph describing one of the main characters. How did you visualize him/her?
- In your own words, describe the setting where most of the action took place. Include a quote from the text to support your answer.
- Which scene or major event in the text was easiest to visualize? Include evidence from the book to support your answer.

Determining Importance

- What was the main problem or conflict in the story? How was it solved?
- What are some things you learned by reading the text that you did not know before?
- What was the most important event in the story? Find three things that caused this event.

Questioning

- What is a really important question that you had while reading? Did you find the answer? If not, how can you find it?
- Create a chart of questions you had before, during, and after reading.
- If you were to write to the author, what questions would you like to ask him/her? Why do you want to know the answers?

Connecting

- Does this text remind you of a current world event? Explain, using specific examples from the text and events from the world.
- Does this text remind you of another text you have read? What are the similarities and differences between the texts?
- Describe a time when you felt like a person in the text. Use details from the text and your own ideas to explain your thinking.

Inferring

- What character trait do you think was the most important for the main character to have? Use examples from the text to explain how he/she showed this trait.
- How does the main character change from the beginning of the book to the end? Use examples from the book and your own ideas to explain your thinking.
- What do you think is the main idea or lesson that can be learned from the text? Use evidence from the text and your own ideas to explain your thinking.

Pembroke Publishers © 2012 *100 Minutes* by Lisa Donohue ISBN 978-1-55138-276-0

Create Your Own Reading-Response Tasks, cont'd

Synthesizing

- Think about an important decision one of the characters had to make in the book. What factors influenced this decision? Do you agree with the decision the character made?
- How would the story have been different if it was told from another character's perspective?
- If you were the author, what might you have changed in the book? Was there more information that you needed about a particular thing? Were there questions that you feel were left unanswered?

HOT

- How do you know that the main character learned an important lesson through the book?
- Do you think the ending is fair to all the characters?
- What do you think motivated the author to write this text?
- Which character do you think was the hero? Why?
- Which character do you think was most important to the plot? Why?
- If you were the main character, how might you have tried to solve the problem?
- Do you agree with the decisions made by the main character?
- What are some of the traits you admire most about one of the characters in the story?
- If this was a real person, would you choose him/her as a friend? Why or why not?
- What is the most important lesson that the author wants us to learn from the book? How do you know this?

Pembroke Publishers © 2012 *100 Minutes* by Lisa Donohue ISBN 978-1-55138-276-0

PART THREE

Writing, Reflecting, and Feedback

A Look at Writing Time

As the students gather on the carpet, the teacher begins by reminding them about the mentor text that they have read together the day before. She asks them to recall some of the features that made it a strong sample of work. The students take a few minutes to turn and talk with their talk-partners, recalling the details of the piece of writing. After a few moments, the teacher invites students to share their thinking with the whole group. One student remembers that the story had very descriptive details, another recalls various elements of the narrative, and another begins to describe the climax with great excitement.

The teacher captures the students' ideas and begins to make a list of the things that made a successful story:

- The story had really good ideas and they were in an order that made sense.
- It had all parts of a good story (characters, setting, plot).
- The plot was really exciting—it had an introduction, problem, challenge, climax, and resolution.
- The writing was really descriptive; it had lots of details.
- The story was very creative and exciting.
- There was an important message/lesson at the end of the story.

Flipping the chart paper, the teacher reveals a story she has started to write:

A long time ago, in a castle far away lived a young wizard. Unfortunately, he always slept during his lessons. The old wizard who was his teacher warned him that he needed to pay more attention.

One day, the young wizard accidentally cast a spell on the castle dragon and caused him to catch a cold and start sneezing.

The young wizard cast another spell and accidentally opened the gates of the castle. The dragon escaped and flew over the village, sneezing fireballs at the houses.

The old wizard cast a rain spell to put out all the fires. The dragon couldn't fly in the rain, and was captured and returned to the castle.

The young wizard got in trouble, and promised to pay more attention in class. He learned how to make a new potion to cure the dragon's cold.

After reading the story aloud, the teacher asks the students to comment on the things they noticed about the story. As a class, they engage in a rich conversation about what was done well and what was potentially missing from the story. The students determine that, although the story has an exciting plot, there are very few descriptive details. Agreeing with the students, the teacher then tasks the students with adding more description to the story. Students are invited to work on their own or with a partner, to choose a part of the story and rewrite it using descriptive writing. After identifying students who choose to work on their own, the remaining students quickly form partners or groups of three.

They disperse into the classroom: some at desks, some sprawled on the floor, and others sitting on the carpet. Each student or group chooses a small part of the story and begins to write it in a way that creates vivid images for the reader. Rich conversations erupt and fill the classroom with engaging, purposeful talk.

After a while, the students return to the carpet. When they are invited to share, the students eagerly read their writing. The teacher begins to add description to the story on the chart paper, crossing out words and inserting others, squeezing in phrases and adding new sentences in the margin. The writing begins to take on the appearance of a revised working copy filled with additions, changes, and revisions.

At last, the class pauses to admire their handiwork. The teacher reminds the students of their collective goal to add descriptive writing to their work. Reading the story aloud, she asks them to determine if they were successful in reaching this goal. Unanimously, the class says that they have indeed succeeded.

Here is the final story:

Once upon a time in a dark forest, there was an ancient castle. Inside the castle lived a young wizard who was learning how to make spells. The young wizard always slept during his spell lessons. The old wizard who was his teacher would spot him sleeping and roughly wake him up. "Young wizard, you must pay more attention in class!"

One day, the young wizard was fooling around in the castle lair. He opened a cupboard and discovered three potions inside.

"I can use these," he said to himself, as he snatched them out.

He got a big, humongous cauldron and mixed them all together. Suddenly, he heard something snoring beside him.

"I've got an idea. I'll test it on the castle dragon," laughed the young wizard.

The young wizard put one drop on the dragon, who immediately started sneezing.

"Oh no!" said the young wizard in a panic. Grabbing other potions, he frantically began a new mixture. The castle gates burst open. The dragon flew out, sneezing fireballs and fire tornadoes.

The young wizard saw that the dragon had sneezed so much that the whole village was on fire and the villagers were running out of their straw houses.

The old wizard looked out of his castle window and saw the entire village on fire. He cast a rain spell, putting out the burning fires. The rain was so heavy that the dragon couldn't fly. Fortunately, the fire-breathing dragon was captured and returned to the castle.

The young wizard got in trouble for making the gates open and giving the dragon a cold. He promised the old wizard that he would pay more attention in class from then on. Later that day, he learned how to make a potion to make the dragon's cold go away forever!
THE END

5

Writing Around the Literacy Block

Writing is a complex process—the Writing Time you have carved out of the literacy block will provide you with an opportunity to provide students with direct instruction in order to help them learn the necessary skills. This time can be used for modelling new forms of writing; exploring mentor texts and determining success criteria; mini-grammar lessons or instruction on parts of speech or word patterns; teaching students how to select topics for writing, to brainstorm, and to organize their ideas; developing a personal writer's voice; and much more. Through direct instruction, teachers are able to provide the framework for students to explore their writing through their independent writing time. The direct-instruction Writing Time should be intentionally connected to the writing that students are doing during their independent writing. In this way, students are being provided with regular times to practice the skills that are being explicitly taught through the lessons. This daily instructional time provides teachers with an opportunity to provide whole-class instruction.

Direct Instruction in Writing

Cunningham and Allington (2003) state, "Students need instruction, guidance, support, encouragement and acceptance if they are going to be willing and able participants in writing." Direct-instruction Writing Time is when teachers can model the numerous skills that good writing encompasses. Research indicates that teachers need to model thinking and composing strategies when teaching writing. Modelled, shared, and guided activities provide students with the support they need to write independently (Bereiter & Scardamalia, 1987; Hillcocks, 1995). Through this whole-class time, teachers can teach a range of skills associated with proficient writing: it can be used to explore different text forms and purposes for writing; to give focused instruction on the various components of the writing process; to provide an opportunity to help students gain an insight into the craft of writing, including voice and style; or as a time to brainstorm and share potential topics or ideas for writing.

As any author will tell you, writing is a messy process. It includes brainstorming, drafting, and lots and lots of revision. Through direct instruction, students not only can explore mentor texts that are copy perfect, but also have an opportunity to witness the down-and-dirty craft of creating pieces of writing. The teacher can serve as an expert writer, modelling the various forms of writing as well as the process of writing. When students are able to understand the thinking processes associated with writing, they are better able to apply these strategies to their own writing.

Nancie Atwell (2003) asks, "The real question for writing teachers...how do we help our students develop a repertoire of approaches to writing that are comparable to reading strategies?...How do we help writers identify problems, solve them, take charge of their writing and thinking?" Through rich whole-class learning opportunities, the teacher is able to help students learn how to organize thoughts, solve problems, reflect on their writing, explore different perspectives, and consider various purposes and audiences for their writing. This time can be used for the teacher to model various aspects of writing, for students to write collaboratively with their peers on shared writing pieces, or for students to share their writing with others, providing and receiving feedback. This time should be used as a flexible opportunity for teaching and learning. It could be as focused as explicitly teaching one specific element of punctuation (e.g., how to use quotation marks) or as broad as providing talk-time for students to discuss ideas related to potential writing topics. It could be used for modelling, sharing, or collaborating. This valuable teaching time helps students understand the metacognitive processes associated with writing. It allows them an opportunity to observe an "expert" writer in action, and engage in rich conversations about writing. It provides the framework that their independent writing time will build on.

The Power of Talk

During Writing Time, students should have frequent opportunities to engage in conversations with each other. This talk can take the form of examining mentor texts in order to determine success criteria, brainstorming collaboratively, or sharing a piece of writing and giving or receiving feedback with their peers. When students are given time to think about their ideas and have an opportunity to share them orally, they meet with greater success in writing them down. Using whole-class Writing Time as a vehicle for teaching leads students to understand forms of writing, to determine the purpose and audience for their pieces, and to share their thinking aloud; these skills will have a significant impact on students during their independent writing during AWARD Time. Students will be more apt to use their writing time productively, having had time previously to think about potential ideas for writing.

Beginning with the End in Mind

The Write Beginning (Donohue, 2009) presents a more comprehensive discussion of constructing success criteria for various forms of writing.

There was a time when my students would ask, "Why didn't I get an A on this?" Often I found myself scrambling to justify a grade and desperately trying to explain which elements might have been missing from the piece of work. Fortunately, that question seems to have disappeared from my students' minds, because they no longer need me to justify their marks—instead, they are able to articulate their own learning goals, successes, and areas for continued improvement. When students become reflective learners, they are much more able to understand the requirements of various tasks and articulate their learning in terms of these targets.

When they are taught to begin with the end in mind, students are able to develop a clear understanding of expectations and learning outcomes, as well as the ways in which they will demonstrate their learning. This allows them to understand the way their work will be assessed, and to perceive their work as purposeful, valuable, and authentic. As young writers, they need to understand their learning target, identify the components that make the writing successful, and receive feedback along the way.

When we involve students in setting the learning targets, they become active participants rather than passive observers in the assessment process. This allows for ongoing dialogue between students and teacher—there are no surprises when it comes to assessment. Students have a clear understanding of the target, and they are able to describe what they need to do in order to reach it. When you involve students in understanding the criteria for success and actively participating in creating the tools with which they will be evaluated, it enables them to have a clear understanding of the skills they are learning, as well as the way in which they will be assessed.

Anne Davies (2008) believes that, in order to support learning, classroom assessment needs to involve students in the assessment process by providing specific descriptive feedback during the learning. Students need to know what they already know, what they need to learn, and what it will look like when they can do it. Being involved in the setting of success criteria, they are able to use it to guide their own learning by setting personal learning goals, collecting evidence of their learning, and sharing their learning with others.

When we involve students in this ongoing assessment process, they become self-reflective self-monitoring learners who assume more responsibility for their learning. They show greater engagement and a deeper understanding of their strengths and needs as learners. They are able to articulate their learning and use assessment as a tool from which they can continue to learn, rather than seeing it as a final summative evaluation. This allows them to point out the features in their work that they think are strong and to set goals for their continued growth. No longer do they ask, "Why didn't I get an A on this?" Instead, students are able to explain for themselves the things they did well and the things they will continue to work on.

Setting Success Criteria

The Writing Time in the 100 Minutes allows for students and teachers to engage in rich dialogues about writing. The time students spend exploring different forms of writing is a perfect chance for them to examine different writing samples and share their observations. Conferencing with small groups through AWARD Time is the best place to provide individual students with feedback, while setting success criteria should be completed as a whole-class activity. In this way, everyone is on the same page when it comes to the learning goals for each form of writing.

Through the use of mentor texts, exemplars, or modelled writing, students are able to develop a clear understanding of the learning goals for their writing. Students and teacher work together to co-construct a list of features that make the work successful—the success criteria. The success criteria are the targets students set for their own writing that will ultimately serve as a tool to assess their work. Success criteria can include targets relating to the form of the writing, the ideas included in the writing, the way the writing is communicated, and the way the students use their writing to apply their knowledge, skills, or interests.

As a way of bringing learning targets into focus for students, teachers might find mentor texts, student exemplars, and teacher modelling valuable tools. Students can use these samples as a way of deconstructing various pieces of writing and establishing the success criteria.

MENTOR TEXTS

Mentor texts are any pieces of writing that clearly demonstrate high levels of success in the skills we are striving to develop in our students. They might include a picture book by a favorite author, an article in the newspaper, a report that was posted on the Internet, or even a letter that has been included in a textbook. A mentor text needs to include recognizable text features and clear ideas. It should be at an appropriate level for students to read and try to emulate, as well as being of a manageable length. These texts should be short, effective, and clear.

The mentor text can be shared with the students through Writing Time. You might choose to read the text with the class or allow students to read the text together in partners or learning groups. While examining the mentor text, students should be encouraged to note the elements of the text that make it a successful piece of writing. They might consider the specific form of the piece, the style of the writing, the voice of the author, the content of the writing, or any other specific features that relate to the focus for instruction:

- Which text form did it follow?
- What are the text features the author uses most effectively?
- How does the author develop ideas?
- How does the author use descriptive writing and clear evidence to support his/her work?
- What is the author's main message?
- How does the author make his/her message clear?
- What connections does the author make through his/her writing?
- What research do you think the author did to write this piece?
- What do you notice about the author's voice through the writing?
- Which part of the writing stands out the most?
- How does the author organize the content?

As students explore the text and share their ideas through discussion, you can help draw their attention to specific features of the piece that are important for them to notice. Through the exploration of text and the rich dialogue they engage in, students begin to develop a familiarity with the text form and are able to use their understanding of the mentor text as a guide for their own writing.

As a whole class, determine which features of the writing are the most important, and use these to form the basis of the success criteria. When students share ideas, ensure that the success criteria are relevant and accurate. Although the students might make numerous interesting observations about the mentor text, the success criteria should reflect the focus for instruction. As a teacher, you will guide the discussion so that students notice the specific elements that are important and can be used to support their writing. At all times, keep the learning goals for the students in mind as, with your students, you co-construct success criteria that will directly support the curriculum expectations for each set of learners.

By participating in rich dialogues and a critical analysis of mentor texts, students are able to engage in rich thinking about the piece of writing. Their conversations will enable them to examine the text on a deeper level. The success criteria can be used by students during their writing as a way of monitoring their own work, and can also serve as a basis for feedback and further goal-setting when conferencing with you. By using Writing Time as a way of constructing success criteria, students develop a common understanding of the expectations of the writing task and are able to use these targets as they work independently or to provide feedback for each other.

EXEMPLARS

Exemplars are samples of student work. They can be very powerful tools, helping students understand the difference between high and low levels of work. Many students enjoy deconstructing samples of writing from other students. It is best, however, to use samples that are not from the current group of students, to ensure an environment where students are free to take risks and explore their own writing with confidence.

Students can examine various samples in order to determine the differences between high-level work and low-level work. When provided with strong and weak samples of writing, students can attempt to rank or order the pieces. If they are encouraged to do this collaboratively with a partner, they will engage in rich conversations justifying their choices. They might think about which elements make some samples strong or what is lacking in the weaker samples. A helpful guiding question may be *What does the strongest sample have that the weakest sample does not?* This helps students focus on the differences between the pieces.

If students are able to examine multiple strong samples, then they might notice specific features from each piece that helped to make it successful, or they could look for commonalities between the successful pieces of writing. For example, they might notice that all the pieces have well-developed ideas that are connected to the topic; they could notice that one piece has exceptional voice, whereas another has creative ideas. Once students have has an opportunity to explore the various samples, they can share their observations through a whole-class discussion to establish the success criteria.

Asking guiding questions can help lead students' attention to specific important elements of the writing. It is important that you keep the intended learning targets in mind and help direct conversations in a way that will allow students to focus on the features that will be useful to them. For example, when exploring exemplars of a report, you might find it helpful to draw students' attention to key features by asking them to notice the way the ideas have been organized; to identify which supporting evidence is most effective; to notice which voice the author uses; to explore how the introduction and the conclusion are connected. By scaffolding students' thinking while exploring exemplars, you can guide students in coming to the desired conclusions. This inductive model of instruction is highly effective, as students feel like they have discovered the keys to success themselves.

The students' observations can serve as the basis for developing the success criteria. As you record students' ideas, point out specific features of the piece and discuss the ways in which the author included them in the writing. In this way, you guide the students in noticing the important features that will become the focus for their own writing, their feedback, and their assessment.

MODELLING

Teacher modelling is a powerful tool for young writers. In the same way that modelled reading allows us to explicitly share the processes we use when reading, modelled writing allows us to demonstrate the strategies we use as writers— our thoughts and the way we overcome the challenges in getting them down in writing. Modelled writing helps students develop an understanding of not only the elements of writing, but also the craft of writing. Through this process, they can see the ways in which a good writer organizes ideas, experiments with words, and uses the writer's voice in different ways for various forms of writing.

A piece of writing that is constructed through teacher modelling can also be used as a mentor text from which the students can construct success criteria. Students can identify the various text features, skills, and strategies that are used throughout the piece. They can record their observations on sticky notes and stick them on the modelled piece, or you might choose to highlight yourself the areas of the writing that demonstrate specific skills that the students need to notice. As students identify the important elements of the piece, you can use their observations to form the basis for the success criteria.

As you model, you are able to draw the students' attention to various elements important to their own writing. As the success criteria are constructed, you can discuss which strategies were used to get the desired results and what the writer was thinking while crafting the piece. This insight into a writer's mind is helpful for young authors. It helps them to understand that writing is the result of an internal dialogue and a reflective thought process that the writer uses to find just the right word or phrase, to organize ideas so that they are clear to the reader.

From Writing Time to Independent Writing

Writing Time is a perfect time to introduce students to new forms of writing. By examining mentor texts, students are able to engage in rich dialogues and identify the elements that make each piece successful. Through these experiences and conversations, students become familiar with the form of writing, then are able to apply this knowledge when writing independently. This ensures that, when students are working on their own writing, their time is well spent. They know what they need to be working on and have had an opportunity to see the writing in action. They have deconstructed mentor texts, ranked student exemplars, or observed a good writer in action. These whole-class activities provide the background knowledge that students can apply through their independent writing, use as a basis for their feedback, and employ to set and monitor personal writing goals. Through exposure to sample texts and the development of success criteria, students develop a clear understanding of the goals for their writing. In order to include the success criteria in their own writing, they need to have a clear understanding of what it looks like in the writing of others.

6

Exploring Different Purposes and Audiences

According to the Ontario Ministry of Education in *The Ontario Curriculum* (2006), students need opportunities to become disciplined thinkers so that they can learn how to communicate their ideas effectively. They need many opportunities to write, because it is through this process that they learn how to select and organize their ideas. They must keep in mind the purpose for which they are writing and the audience for whom the writing is intended. The writing curriculum states:

> Students should be given the kinds of assignments that provide opportunities to produce writing that is interesting and original and reflects their capacity for independent critical thought. Writing activities that students see as meaningful and that challenge them to think creatively about topics and concerns of interest to them will lead to a fuller and more lasting command of the essential skills of writing.

In order for students to become good writers, they need frequent opportunities to write for various purposes and audiences. Through these writing experiences, they learn how to vary their writing style, organization, and voice to suit the purpose and audience for the writing.

Writing Time is a perfect opportunity to introduce students to the various purposes for writing, explore potential audiences for writing, and introduce writing in a range of forms. This time allows teachers to provide direct instruction using mentor texts (such as published pieces), student exemplars, or modelled pieces of writing to help students acquire the knowledge necessary to use their independent writing time in a focused, productive way. As students are introduced to different writing skills, they are able to apply them during AWARD Time. In this way, they can test out the skills they are learning with their own writing, as well as receive immediate feedback on their progress.

When we write, we do so for a variety of purposes. We might write a letter to a friend, share a recipe through an e-mail, or—most dreaded—write report cards to share information with parents. In our lives, we've had to write for a number of different reasons and recognize the purpose and audience of each form of writing without needing to give it much conscious thought. However, most forms of writing can be reflected in the following purposes for writing: we write to inform, to persuade, to reflect, or to entertain. We also write for different audiences: we might write a letter to a friend, create a blog for personal and shared reflection, jot down a to-do list for a spouse, or compose an essay for a professor. When we combine the purpose of writing with the intended audience, we can adjust the form of writing accordingly. For example, we might be asked to write a letter to someone in order to convince them of something. In this light, we would combine the purpose (to convince someone) with the audience (recipient of the letter) to determine the form the writing should take (i.e., a persuasive letter).

After focusing on specific purposes of writing and building an awareness of the audience for the writing, students can use this information to determine the form and voice that their writing should take. When we write to entertain, we might choose to write a narrative; when we write to inform, we could write a report or a procedure; when we write to persuade, we might write a paragraph, letter, or essay; and when we write to reflect, we might write a journal or a blog. We can help students determine the form that their writing needs to take by teaching them to balance the purpose and the audience for each writing task.

For each type of writing, you will find a variety of tools: question prompts to get students thinking about and reflecting on their writing, graphic organizers to help students plan their writing, sample success criteria, and a set of writing prompts.

For a greater variety of writing prompts, see *The Write Voice* (Donohue, 2011).

Using Writing Prompts

Hmmmm, what should I write about? This is a tough question for children and adults alike. Often just getting started is the hardest part. The prospect of deciding on a topic, brainstorming ideas, formulating a plan, and organizing information is enough to give even the most confident writer a block at times. While we can't teach students to be inspired, we can set the stage for inspiration to happen. What is inspiration? Inspiration is the explosion in our mind that starts our creativity flowing. How can we help students to find their own inspiration? Providing meaningful writing tasks and allowing students to have choice in their writing can help them get over the block that sometimes comes with writing.

Artifact Box as Inspiration

Students benefit from experiential learning. In order for them to write, they need to have sufficient background knowledge. They need to be able to draw on their prior experiences to create vibrant mental images for their readers or create a convincing argument from a certain perspective. All students bring a wealth of personal experiences, opinions, and perspectives to each classroom. However, they might not be able to recall certain details at a moment's notice. They might forget specific details or be unable to recall elements that could help to build a realistic image in their reader's mind.

An Artifact Box is a tool that can help students use tangible objects as a way of connecting to their prior experiences and unlocking their creativity. This box would contain a number of different items that students can use as a source of inspiration for their writing. What would happen if students discovered an old key in the artifact box? They would automatically be filled with a wide range of questions: Where did it come from? What do you think it unlocks? What secret do you think it is hiding? How can we find the lock it opens? Are there any clues on the key that might help in discovering what it might unlock? Who might own the treasure behind the lock? Should we keep it a secret; why or why not?

Other ideas for an Artifact Box:

- Lost-pet poster
- Old lamp/jar/container
- Quill pen
- Torn sports jersey
- Old road map
- Cell phone
- Used boarding pass
- Holiday brochure
- Old-fashioned family portrait
- Newspaper clipping (classified ad, headline, etc.)
- Costume jewelry

During Writing Time, students are introduced to different items to be placed in the artifact box or share items that they have contributed for the class. Students might need time to explore the items and think about the stories they hold. These discussions can take place during Writing Time; the teacher might choose to model writing using an artifact as a source of inspiration. Providing time for students to explore the artifact box prior to and during AWARD Time can help the ones who are struggling with writer's block find a new and creative source of inspiration.

You might consider copying the writing ideas onto cardstock and placing them in a place where the students can easily access them.

One strategy to use when introducing students to different writing ideas is to have them use Writing Time to explore different writing prompts. For example, if students are learning how to write narratives, you could begin by asking them to sit with their talk-partners. Begin by reading one of the writing ideas (found on pages between 90 and 101) to the whole class; for example, the Entertaining Ideas are suitable prompts for students to use when writing narratives. After reading the prompt, allow at least 20–30 seconds for students to do some independent thinking. They then take a few minutes and share their ideas with their talk-partners. During this pre-writing discussion, students can be presented with different aspects of the narrative to think and talk about; for example, you might say, "For the next prompt, think about the setting; where would a story like this take place?" or "When I read the prompt, think about the conflict in the story; how would the problem be created?" or "After listening to the prompt, think about who might be involved in the story."

Scaffolding the students' writing by allowing them time to think and talk before writing will help them select writing topics, gather ideas, and organize their thinking in order to optimize their AWARD Time. If students have been introduced to a variety of writing prompts and have had an opportunity to think about them, they will be less likely to face the dreaded writer's block during their independent writing time.

Writing prompts help students generate ideas for their writing. They should never be used to limit students' creativity. Students should be encouraged to use writing prompts as a way of inspiring their own writing and thinking of additional potential topics for writing. Students can add to the existing bank of writing prompts or collect pictures that can serve as catalysts for creativity. The more ideas students can contribute, the more authentic and relevant their writing will become. The writing prompts included in the book are broad and general in an

On pages between 90 and 101 are some writing prompts to help get the writing started. They are simple writing ideas that allow students to explore four purposes of writing: to inform, to persuade, to reflect, and to entertain. For example, if the students are learning about how to write persuasively, they may find the HOT Topics helpful; if they were writing narratives, the Entertaining Ideas might help spark their creativity.

While the prompts hardly address all the forms of writing, they might be helpful for students when they are trying to get started with their writing.

attempt to reach as wide an audience as possible; they are meant suggestions and supports. Each class will have different interests and this should be reflected in the writing topics generated for them. As teachers are the experts on their own students they should select the writing prompts they think might best inspire their students, and then work with their students to brainstorm and create additional potential writing ideas. The more time we invest in helping students find their own writing topics, ideas, and inspiration, the more engaged they will be in the writing process.

Inspiration is found through choice—if students have an opportunity to browse through different writing ideas, they can select one they are passionate about or that helps them formulate their own ideas. Select the writing topics that best support the type of instruction that is taking place during Writing Time. You might decide to use writing ideas from Recall and Reflect when teaching students how to write recounts, or possibly Inform Me! when teaching students about report writing; you might find the writing ideas in HOT Topics perfect for writing expositions, and the Entertaining Ideas could help when writing narratives.

While this book provides a number of writing prompts, nothing replaces brainstorming ideas with your own students. They bring their own experiences, knowledge, and opinions to the classroom, so consider your students' wealth of knowledge and personal interests as a foundation for new writing ideas. Involve students in the creation of potential writing ideas that can be added to their choices to consider when writing.

For simplicity's sake, consider creating a space in the classroom where the writing ideas can be kept. You might create an Inspiration Box and place the writing ideas on recipe cards sorted into different sections; you might create a system where the writing ideas are housed in pockets stapled to a bulletin board. With younger students, you could introduce a few writing ideas at a time during the Writing Time and allow them to brainstorm ideas with their talk-partners. This way, when they choose a topic they will already have had an opportunity to think and talk about the ideas they would like to write about. With older students, consider introducing three or four writing ideas at a time and providing them with some time to think and talk with their talk-partners about which one(s) they might consider writing. Students can tuck cards that they find interesting into their writing books to serve as inspiration during their independent writing. When you introduce students to writing ideas during the whole-class Writing Time, they are well-prepared for their independent writing. They can then use their AWARD Time for actually writing, knowing that they have already taken the time to think and talk about their ideas.

Write to Reflect

Writing to reflect allows the writer time to recount various events and consider their significance. This writing can take the form of a journal, a diary, or a recount. Typically, students present nonfiction information about a personal experience in sequential order; i.e., describing events in the order that they happened.

The following is a list of questions you might find helpful when introducing students to reflective writing, either during Writing Time or in writing conferences. These questions might help students generate ideas or reflect on their writing:

• What do you want your reader to know about this experience?

- How did you feel about it?
- What words will you include that will help the reader understand your thoughts and feelings?
- How can you use sequencing words (e.g., *first, then, finally*) to organize your ideas?
- Did you learn an important lesson through this event?
- What do you want your reader to continue thinking about after reading your writing?
- Are there parts that you can describe vividly?
- How can you use your five senses to describe the event?
- How do you want your reader to feel after reading your writing?
- What words can you use that will help give the reader a good mental image of the event you are describing?
- Which parts are the most important? Are there any parts that you could leave out that are irrelevant?
- Are there any parts that are more important than others? How will you draw your reader's attention to these parts?

A Caution About Privacy

The audience for a journal can be public or private. When we write to reflect, we might be writing to share our personal experiences with others or to help ourselves better understand the things that happen in our lives. There are times when keeping a journal can help us work through different events in our lives; the value from these journals comes from the process of writing, rather than the product that is derived. Some people find this kind of journaling therapeutic, as it helps them gain a better understanding into their own thinking. However, this kind of reflective writing should be kept private and used only for the purpose of "thinking through writing." If students choose to keep personal journals at home, these writings need to be respected as private personal reflections. Unfortunately, at times students have mistaken blogs or other public forums as appropriate places to post their private personal reflections. Just as we need to encourage students to have a safe private forum to reflect on their own lives, we also need to help them develop an awareness of which reflections are best kept private, which can be shared with a select audience, and which are suitable for sharing publically. With the ease of communication of the digital age comes the need to help students distinguish between public and private information. Engaging in conversations about the intended audience for reflections is essential, so that students can develop an awareness of the differences between reflections that can be shared and those that should be kept private.

We might ask students to reflect through a variety of forms or for different audiences. If we ask students to write for the purpose of reflecting, they need to know that their entries are not private and will be shared with an audience; this might alter the content and form of the writing.

SAMPLE SUCCESS CRITERIA FOR REFLECTIVE WRITING

I am learning how to write to REFLECT:

- My writing will describe an event or series of events in chronological order or a sequence that makes sense.

- My writing will have a main idea and have a focused purpose.
- I will provide information about who, what, when, where, why, and how the event happened.
- My writing will help to show how I have reflected on a personal experience.
- I will include details that describe how I felt and what I thought.
- I will describe the event using my five senses.
- I will use sequencing words (e.g., *first*, *then*, *finally*), to help organize my ideas and share them in a logical sequential order.
- I will use a writing voice and style that reflects my personality.
- I will show how my experiences are connected to my thoughts and feelings.
- My writing will demonstrate how an experience taught me an important lesson.

USING THE GRAPHIC ORGANIZER AND PROMPT CARDS

You might find the graphic organizer on page 89 helpful for students to use when planning their reflections.

Pages 90 and 91 contain suggestions of topics that students can choose from. As with all writing activities, teachers should use the interests of each class in order to determine appropriate writing topics. The suggestions can help get students started, but teachers might find more value in brainstorming possible writing topics with their class.

Write to Entertain

When writers write for the purpose of entertaining, they typically write using creativity and their imagination. This often takes the form of narrative writing. Narrative writing tells a story, and consists of the basic elements of a plot, characters, and a setting. While creating stories, young writers can develop their personal writing voice by experimenting with character development, use of sensory statements, creative word usage, and emotional cues. These all work together to develop an author's sense of style and ultimately the writer's voice.

> **Voice-Building Strategies**
>
> **Emotional Cues** – Using emotional connections to build mood
> **Sensory Statements** – Using the five senses to help readers create a mental image
> **Wordsmithing** – Building vocabulary and promoting risk-taking with creative word use
> **Perspective** – Understanding that the person telling the story is as important as the story itself
> **Character Development** – Setting the stage for action by creating interesting characters with voices of their own
> **Style** – Understanding how writing conventions, literary devices, and presentation techniques can be used to strengthen voice
> (Donohue, 2011)

You might find the following questions helpful when introducing students to narrative writing during the Writing Time of the literacy block or when conferencing with students about their writing:

- What is the problem/conflict in your writing?
- How can you capture your readers' attention at the beginning?

You might copy some of the writing ideas and add them to an Inspiration Box or an interactive bulletin board. During independent writing time, students can select a topic they would like to write about. This greatly reduces writer's block and allows students to maximize their writing time.

For more on helping students develop their own voice in their writing, see *The Write Voice* (Donohue, 2011).

- How can you create a mood of suspense/humor/joy/empathy through your writing?
- Do you need any sequencing or time-order words (e.g., *first*, *then*, *after*, *finally*) to help clarify the sequence of events in your writing?
- Are there any words or sentences in your writing that make the reader understand how you (or the characters) are feeling?
- How can you help the reader make a picture of this in their mind?

SAMPLE SUCCESS CRITERIA FOR WRITING TO ENTERTAIN

I am learning how to write to ENTERTAIN:

- My writing includes a well-developed plot (including introduction, problem, challenge, climax, and resolution).
- I will make sure that my ideas are introduced in a logical sequential way.
- I will organize my ideas so that my writing flows clearly.
- I will create visual images for the reader.
- I will include enough information to make the story fit together.
- I will use descriptive words and details to make my writing come alive.
- I will use my imagination and include creative ideas.
- I will use my writing voice and word choice to enhance my ideas.
- I will try to develop an overall theme, moral, lesson, or purpose in my writing.
- My writing will be the best that I can make it—including correct spelling, punctuation, and grammar.

USING THE GRAPHIC ORGANIZER AND PROMPT CARDS

The graphic organizer shown here is part of an app on Toontastic. Toontastic is a "Creative Learning app for the iPad that empowers kids to draw, animate, and narrate their own cartoons and share them with friends & family around the world." Using this app, children are introduced to the elements of a plotline, including Setup, Conflict, Challenge, Climax, and Resolution. Through play, children can create cartoons that have sophisticated story lines. The graphic organizer on page 92 uses a similar structure to assist students organize their ideas and transfer this structure to their story writing.

Screenshot reproduced with permission from Toontastic

For a greater variety of writing prompts suitable for narrative writing, see *The Write Voice* (Donohue, 2011)

Pages 93–94 contain writing prompts that students might find helpful when beginning to develop their ideas. You can place these prompts in a location that students can easily access during independent writing times.

Write to Inform

Informative writing can take many different forms: it can be a report, a recipe, an essay, a website, or one of many other nonfiction texts. When writing to inform, the writer's intent is to share information with the reader. The information the writer shares might be a combination of personal experiences, prior knowledge, and facts learned through research or other sources.

When teaching students to write informative pieces, it makes sense to integrate media literacy and critical literacy. This is a perfect time to introduce students to the challenges of evaluating the accuracy of information that they encounter, especially if they are using online sources. They need to consider the source of information and to learn strategies for verifying information. Also, this could be an appropriate time to introduce students to the importance of citing sources, the correct way in which information is quoted or shared, and the dangers of plagiarism. Informational writing is the form of writing that students will probably use the most as they progress through school, and therefore it is highly beneficial for students to begin to develop their informational-writing skills as early as possible.

You might find these questions helpful when introducing students to informational writing during Writing Time or when conferencing with students during Writing Conferences:

- How can you find information about your topic?
- How will you organize your information?
- What information can you group together to create paragraphs? How will you organize the paragraphs so they flow in the most logical sequence?
- Do you know enough about the topic? If not, where will you find more information?
- How do you know if the information you have found is accurate and relevant? Can you trust your sources? How will you cite the sources that you used?
- Are you keeping a record of where you found your information?
- How can you capture your reader's attention at the beginning?
- What do you want your readers to continue thinking about after they have read your writing?
- Does all your information support your main idea? Is it all connected to your main idea? Is it relevant, specific, and accurate?
- Do any of your sources have conflicting information? How will you determine which source is most accurate?
- How might you share your work with your classmates?
- Is there someone you consider an expert in this subject who might be able to help you gather and organize your ideas?

SAMPLE SUCCESS CRITERIA FOR INFORMATIVE WRITING

I am learning how to write to INFORM:

- My writing will include an introduction and a conclusion that clearly states my main idea.
- I will include information that helps the reader develop a clear understanding of the topic.
- I will include relevant facts that show *who*, *what*, *where*, *when*, *why*, and *how*.
- My writing will include interesting content and supporting details.
- I will organize my ideas so they are presented in a logical sequential manner.

- I will use vocabulary that is appropriate and relevant for the subject.
- I will use descriptive words, phrases, and ideas when possible.
- My writing will be organized into paragraphs.
- I can use different sources to collect background information for my writing.
- I will include quotes when necessary and cite information I found from other sources.
- I will evaluate which information is important and which information is irrelevant.

USING THE GRAPHIC ORGANIZER AND PROMPT CARDS

The graphic organizer on page 95 and the writing prompts on page 96 might help students generate ideas and collect information about their topics.

Write to Convince

When we write to convince, we are attempting to persuade the reader through our writing. To do this, we need to clearly state a point of view, an opinion, or a belief and then defend or justify it. The more logical our rationale, the more convincing our writing will be. When we ask students to form a judgment and then justify it, we are asking them to apply higher-order thinking skills. We are asking them to think critically and present a reasonable rationale to justify their ideas. In order to be critical thinkers, students need to be able to analyze information, evaluate possibilities, compare options, and effectively communicate their thinking. Critical thinking is not about having the correct answer, but instead about having a reasonable answer that can be justified. Students need to draw on their previous experiences and their prior knowledge in order to build a plausible answer. They need to be able to state an opinion and then justify their thinking by using evidence in the form of examples from their own lives, information they have read, or knowledge they have gained from reliable sources.

Writing to convince demands that students state their idea and then justify their thinking. Students can demonstrate this writing skill in a variety of forms ranging from a simple paragraph to a more-complex essay. Basically, the principles remain the same: State an idea, opinion, or thesis; prove it using reliable sources of information (e.g., personal experiences, information, research if necessary).

You might use the following questions when introducing students to persuasive writing during Writing Times or when conferencing with students during Writing Conferences:

- What is your opinion on the subject?
- How will you convince others to agree with your point of view?
- What evidence can you use to support your opinion?
- How can you best organize your ideas so that they support your opinion?
- Are there words/phrases you can use to help clarify or express your opinion?
- What do you want readers to think about after they have read your writing?
- What is a reliable source you might use to find out more information about this subject?
- How can you verify the reliability and accuracy of the sources you have consulted?
- Are there sources you should cite or reference in your writing?
- Is there a possible counter-argument? How can you address it?

SAMPLE SUCCESS CRITERIA FOR PERSUASIVE WRITING

I am learning how to write to PERSUADE:

- In my writing, I will clearly state my idea, suggestion, or opinion.
- I will include sufficient evidence/details to support my opinion.
- My writing will include an introduction and a conclusion that present and summarize the issues.
- Where possible, I can use creative language that helps to express a strong emotion.
- I will organize my ideas in a way that is logical and reasonable.
- The evidence I include will be relevant; I will show how it supports my opinion.
- If there is a counter-argument, I will address it (if possible).
- My writing will have a more formal voice, style, or tone.
- If I have used evidence from different sources, I will check the sources for accuracy and reliability.
- When I include evidence from other sources, I will cite the source of the information.
- My writing will be the best that I can make it, including correct spelling, punctuation, and grammar.

USING THE GRAPHIC ORGANIZER

The graphic organizer on page 97 might be helpful for students to use when planning their writing. Students of all ages can use similar strategies for building a convincing argument; however, the complexity of the ideas and the sophistication of evidence will be reflective of students' age and development.

HOT TOPICS

Pages 98–101 contain suggestions that students might choose to write about. As is the case with all writing activities, use the interests of each class in order to determine appropriate writing topics. The writing prompts can help get students started, but you might find more value in brainstorming possible writing topics with your class. Four boxes on page 101 are left blank for ideas created for your class.

When creating writing topics that elicit higher-order thinking through critical analysis, it is important to remember that students should be challenged to make a choice and then justify that choice. In younger grades the choice could be as simple as *Which animal do you think would make the best class pet?* Older students can be challenged with more sophisticated questions, such as *If you could travel to any event in history, what would you choose to witness first-hand?*

As students are introduced to this form of writing, they need to be aware that there is no one right answer. They need to explore their own thinking and justify their own ideas. Fostering this creativity through critical thinking encourages students to think deeply about different topics and issues.

You can copy some of the writing ideas and add them to an Inspiration Box or interactive bulletin board. During independent writing time, students can select a topic they would like to write about. This greatly reduces writer's block and allows students to maximize their writing time.

Write to Reflect: Recall and Reflect

Recall What happened?	Big Idea:	
Reflect Describe the events sequentially	First...	What feelings/emotions are connected to this event?
	Then...	Which senses can you use to help describe the event/experience fully?
	Finally...	What did you see? What did you hear? What did you smell? What did you touch? What did you taste?

Writing Prompt Cards: Recall and Reflect

RECALL AND REFLECT

Describe the time you were most proud of yourself.

RECALL AND REFLECT

Describe your favorite family vacation.

RECALL AND REFLECT

When did you learn a lesson you will never forget?

RECALL AND REFLECT

Describe a time when you were able to help someone.

RECALL AND REFLECT

What was your favorite trip ever?

RECALL AND REFLECT

Describe a time when you were brave.

Pembroke Publishers © 2012 *100 Minutes* by Lisa Donohue ISBN 978-1-55138-276-0

Writing Prompt Cards: Recall and Reflect

RECALL AND REFLECT

Have you ever won something? Describe what you won and how you won it.

RECALL AND REFLECT

What was the best day of your life?

RECALL AND REFLECT

What was your favorite birthday like?

RECALL AND REFLECT

Describe a time when you learned something new about someone you love.

RECALL AND REFLECT

Describe a person in your life who has been influential. Why were/are they important? What did you learn from them?

RECALL AND REFLECT

Describe a time when you had to face one of your fears. What were you afraid of and how did you overcome it.

Pembroke Publishers © 2012 *100 Minutes* by Lisa Donohue ISBN 978-1-55138-276-0

Write to Entertain: Plotline

Use the following plotline to develop an exciting story.

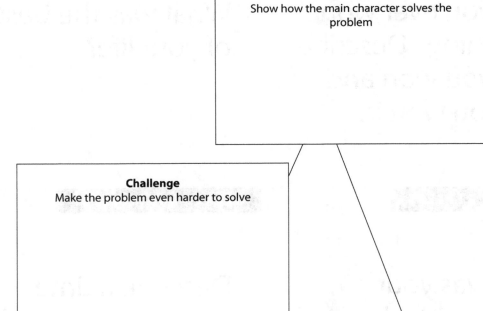

Climax
Show how the main character solves the problem

Challenge
Make the problem even harder to solve

Problem
Introduce the problem the main character will need to solve

Resolution
Show that everything has been resolved or that the lesson has been learned

Introduction
Create a setting and begin to introduce the characters

(Adapted from Toontastic)

Pembroke Publishers © 2012 *100 Minutes* by Lisa Donohue ISBN 978-1-55138-276-0

Writing Prompt Cards: Entertaining Ideas

ENTERTAINING IDEAS

Imagine discovering a treasure from the past. What could you find, and what adventure could it take you on?

ENTERTAINING IDEAS

Imagine discovering a new species of plant or animal. Write about why your discovery is exciting and important.

ENTERTAINING IDEAS

Imagine waking up one morning to find out that your greatest wish has come true. What would your life be like?

ENTERTAINING IDEAS

Imagine discovering that you had magical powers. Write about the adventure this new discovery brings.

ENTERTAINING IDEAS

Imagine discovering a mythical creature. Write about the adventure you have with it.

ENTERTAINING IDEAS

Imagine discovering a time machine. Write about the adventure it takes you on.

Pembroke Publishers © 2012 *100 Minutes* by Lisa Donohue ISBN 978-1-55138-276-0

Writing Prompt Cards: Entertaining Ideas

ENTERTAINING IDEAS

What would happen if you were taken on board an alien spaceship? Where would the aliens take you? What adventures would you have?

ENTERTAINING IDEAS

What would happen if you discovered an ancient key? What would it open? What adventure might it take you on?

ENTERTAINING IDEAS

What might happen if you were stranded on an island? Who would you be with? What might happen while you were there?

ENTERTAINING IDEAS

What might happen if you were invited to spend the night in an ancient castle? What secrets might you discover while you were there?

ENTERTAINING IDEAS

Have you ever had a day when everything seemed to go wrong? Write a humorous adventure about a character who has the worst luck. What kinds of things might go wrong for him/her? What lesson might this character learn in the end?

ENTERTAINING IDEAS

Write an adventure story about a character who comes face-to-face with his/her greatest fear. What might he/she be afraid of? How would the character overcome it?

Pembroke Publishers © 2012 *100 Minutes* by Lisa Donohue ISBN 978-1-55138-276-0

Write to Inform: Web Organizer

Use the following web to organize your information.

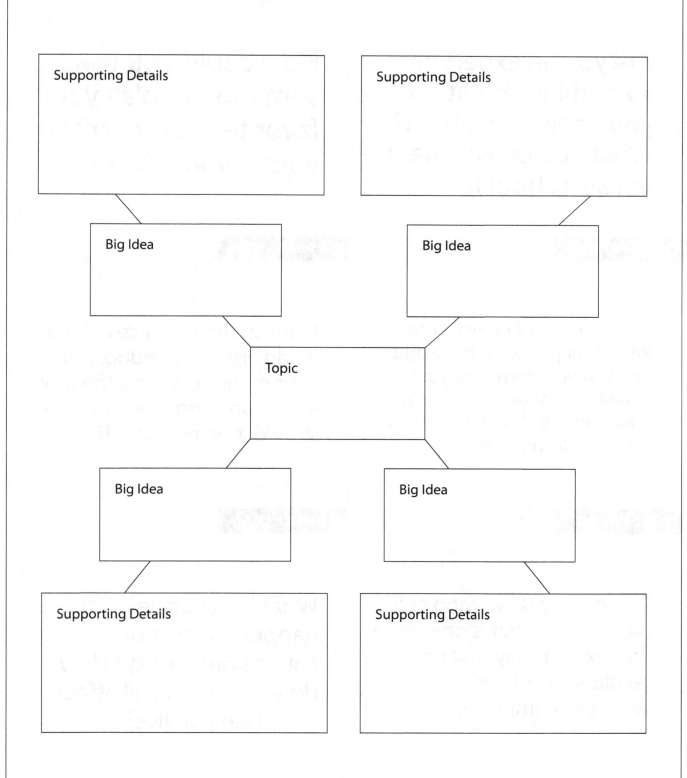

Writing Prompt Cards: Inform Me!

INFORM ME!

Are you an expert in something? What do you know a lot about? What else do you want to learn about it?

INFORM ME!

How could you teach someone to play your favorite sport or make your favorite food?

INFORM ME!

There are lots of powerful and important people in the world today. Who is someone you think has a lot of influence? Write about how and why this person became so important.

INFORM ME!

Many of the resources of the world are being reduced. In your opinion, what is the most important resource and how should it be protected?

INFORM ME!

Technology is evolving at a rapid pace. What is one thing that exists today that has revolutionized our world? Why is it so important?

INFORM ME!

What is a change happening in your community or city? How do you think it will affect the place you live?

Pembroke Publishers © 2012 *100 Minutes* by Lisa Donohue ISBN 978-1-55138-276-0

Write to Convince: Logic Table

Use the following table to organize your ideas.

State What is your Main Idea?	Topic	
Justify How can you prove it?	Big Idea	Supporting Evidence
	Big Idea	Supporting Evidence
	Big Idea	Supporting Evidence
Conclude What can you conclude?	Conclusion	

Writing Prompt Cards: HOT Topic

HOT TOPIC

Which animal would make the best class pet?

HOT TOPIC

If you met someone without any toys, which one of your toys would you share with him/her?

HOT TOPIC

Which is better: the pencil or the computer?

HOT TOPIC

If you could live anywhere in the world, where would you go?

HOT TOPIC

If you could meet anyone (dead or alive) who would you choose?

HOT TOPIC

If your pet could talk, what would you want to know?

Pembroke Publishers © 2012 *100 Minutes* by Lisa Donohue ISBN 978-1-55138-276-0

Writing Prompt Cards: HOT Topic

HOT TOPIC

Who is the person who has had the most influence in your life?

HOT TOPIC

If you could travel to any event in history, what would you choose to witness first-hand?

HOT TOPIC

What would you do if you found something valuable that didn't belong to you?

HOT TOPIC

If you could take one modern invention into the past, what would you take and who would you share it with?

HOT TOPIC

What is something you never seem to have enough time for in your life?

HOT TOPIC

Do you feel that tests are the best way to measure your learning?

Pembroke Publishers © 2012 *100 Minutes* by Lisa Donohue ISBN 978-1-55138-276-0

Writing Prompt Cards: HOT Topic

HOT TOPIC

If you were to create a time capsule, what would you put in it?

HOT TOPIC

If you could plan your next field trip, where would you like to go?

HOT TOPIC

How could you convince someone that it is important to respect the environment?

HOT TOPIC

What would you do if you discovered that your friend was being bullied?

HOT TOPIC

Imagine life in the future? What do you think will be the biggest change?

HOT TOPIC

If your school was given money to start a new program, what program would you like to see started?

Pembroke Publishers © 2012 *100 Minutes* by Lisa Donohue ISBN 978-1-55138-276-0

Writing Prompt Cards: HOT Topic

If you could be any character from a movie or a book, who would you like to be?

If you could train a wild animal as a pet, which animal would you choose?

Pembroke Publishers © 2012 *100 Minutes* by Lisa Donohue ISBN 978-1-55138-276-0

PART FOUR

AWARD Time

A Look at AWARD Time

As AWARD (Applying Writing And Reading Daily) Time starts, the students all seem to go in different directions at once. Pausing to consult the tracking board, they gather the materials they require and set off to their designated tasks...

...**Ravi** gathers his reading-response journal and heads to the conference table. Within a few minutes a few of his classmates meet him there and they begin to share their reading-response tasks from their independent reading texts. The teacher joins them and takes a brief moment to reflect and provide feedback on the completed reading-response tasks. Making a mental note that Ravi has had difficulty finding evidence from the text to prove his answer, she plans to include this in today's guided reading lesson. The teacher conducts a guided reading lesson, challenging Ravi with the question, "How do you know that?" and asking him to put his finger on the part of the text that told him.

After reading a text together, the group is dismissed to their desks. They take the text with them, along with a reading-response task. Ravi, of course, will focus on providing proof for his answers by including either a quote from the text or giving an example to support his thinking. The students spend the next 10 to 15 minutes working on their tasks. The few who finish early eagerly pull out their independent reading books and immediately settle down to read.

... **Marcus** met with the teacher the day before for guided reading and was struggling with the concept of determining importance. As he settles down with his independent reading book, he plans to record three big ideas from this day's reading. His nonfiction book is full of interesting facts and amazing photographs. Before long, he is fascinated with the bizarre and outrageous information contained in his book. As he reads, he consciously tries to decipher the difference between big ideas and supporting details. He pulls out his reading-response journal and flips to the reading-response task he has chosen to complete. He thinks critically about the content of the book and is certain that he is able to identify at least two big ideas. He records them, pausing to think about a third. Flipping the book shut, an idea dawns on him—the cover image and title help him form a third big idea. Satisfied that he has completed his work to the best of his ability, Marcus eagerly returns to his reading. The random facts are too difficult to resist!

...**Emily** pauses, after examining the tracking board, to look at a piece of writing that her teacher modelled for the class the day before. She reads it thoughtfully and then consults the chart with the success criteria. She makes one more stop at the interactive bulletin board, where she selects a familiar HOT topic that she has been curious to explore. She settles at her desk and begins to write. Pausing to reflect on the mentor text and the success criteria, Emily spends her time crafting her ideas into a convincing argument. She glances up and realizes that the students at the guided-reading table are starting to return to their desks, so she takes a few moments to complete her sentence. Just then, she hears the signal that indicates to the class that they should change to their second AWARD task. Emily gathers her work and heads to the conference table. There she is joined by a group of her fellow writers, who have all been diligently crafting persuasive arguments. The teacher invites them to share with each other and provides them with an opportunity to provide feedback to each other. The teacher takes a moment or two to reflect on the writing, ensuring that each student is able to express a personal writing goal. Emily writes hers on the top of her page so that she will be able to refer to it the next day as she continues to work on her writing. When the conference is over, Emily decides that she needs more time to think about what she would like to write next. With a few minutes remaining, she pulls out her independent reading book and settles down to read.

...**Danny** pulls out his writing book and flips to his notes from the day before. After his writing conference, he has decided that he needs to add more supporting details to his argument. His peers were quite helpful in giving him suggestions, which he has now scribbled in the margins of his notebook. Taking a deep breath, he begins to tackle the task of revising his work. He knows that he has solid arguments, that he just needs to back them up with supporting evidence. Danny turns to his graphic organizer and begins to add to it to help organize his thinking. After a few minutes, he is ready to continue his writing. He starts adding sentences where possible and, using his own style of editing, inserting or changing his work as necessary. When the teacher gives the signal for everyone to change to the second task, Danny asks Liya if she could listen to his writing and see if he has effectively added more evidence to his arguments. They head off to a quiet corner of the classroom and engage in a valuable peer conference. Danny respects Liya's opinion and he's happy that she thinks he has made significant improvements to his work. Likewise, Liya asks Danny for his opinion as she shares her writing with him. They are so engaged in their conversation that they don't realize when the teacher indicates that AWARD Time is over.

...**Arthur** can't wait for AWARD Time to begin. He has been watching the schedule in eager anticipation and today is his day, his favorite day in Literacy World. As soon as the teacher indicates that AWARD Time is about to begin, Arthur is halfway across the classroom on his way to the computers. He is eager to work on his advertisement, certain to convince everyone that his product is the best and most important invention in the world. Arthur has chosen to create an entire media blitz, including posters, comic strips, and a full 30-second commercial that is sure to impress. He settles into a focused, engaged trance as his fingers dance across the keyboard. When the teacher gives the signal to change tasks, Arthur smiles, knowing that he has more time to continue working on his media blitz.

...Before beginning AWARD Time **the teacher** has taken a few moments to review the daily tracking board to ensure that all students know which tasks they will be working on and in what order. She reminds the group meeting her for guided reading to bring their reading-response journals and tells all writers to remember to check the success criteria as well as their personal writing goals. The groups are dismissed and they all head to their respective tasks. She notices that Emily has paused to review the modelled writing and that Arthur is so eager that he almost trips over the carpet. By the time the teacher gets to the guided-reading table, Ravi and his group have already gathered and started to share their reading responses. She takes a few moments to review their work, providing them with immediate feedback and making a note of areas that each student needs to continue working on. Ravi is struggling to provide evidence for his answers, but so are three other students in his group, so this will certainly be an instructional focus for today's lesson.

Once the guided-reading lesson has concluded, the teacher gives the signal for the students to change to their second task. She can't help but notice the ear-to-ear grin on Arthur's face!

Emily arrives at the conference table along with the rest of her group. They have all been working on their persuasive writing pieces. Some students have written a lot and some have only started to brainstorm on a graphic organizer. They take turns sharing their writing and their ideas, and the teacher provides each student with immediate feedback. They share ideas about how they can continue to shape their arguments. Each student writes at least one suggestion on the top of his/her page as a reminder of a specific writing goal to continue to work on in his/her writing. Emily has done some really good thinking and has started to organize her ideas in a way that will be effective. She will continue to think about how the organization of her ideas will best support her argument.

The writing conferences are over and the young writers head back to their desks. The teacher looks around and notices Luke. Luke seems to be struggling with his book. The teacher meets Luke at his desk and asks him a few questions about his book. She realizes that it is much too difficult for him, so they quickly head over to the book boxes where together they select a more appropriate text. The teacher encourages Luke to read a few paragraphs to her and she comments on how well his fluency is improving. Luke beams!

The teacher glances at the clock and notices that AWARD Time has come to an end. She signals the class to finish up their tasks and meet together for Writing Time. Arthur is still smiling!

7

The Foundation of Independence

The cornerstone to an effective literacy block is structuring opportunities for small-group instruction. Through these focused groups, teachers can explicitly teach, guide, monitor, observe, and assess individual students' progress. Guided-reading groups provide the opportunity for teachers to listen to students read individually, engage in rich conversations about their thinking about different texts, evaluate students' comprehension, monitor their fluency, strengthen their expression, and more. Similarly, meeting with small groups of students to share and discuss their writing provides opportunities for students to listen to the work of others, receive feedback from each other and the teacher, and set individual writing goals. Through frequent ongoing small-group meetings, the teacher is able to constantly assess each student's learning as well as immediately identify gaps or areas for further growth and development. But, how is it possible for the teacher to meet with students in these small groups for focused instruction? What are the other students in the class doing, while these learning conferences are going on? How can we find time to meet with every student to discuss their reading and writing?

The key to successful small-group instruction is independence, and it begins in the first few days of school. It is within these initial weeks that students need to begin to develop solid routines that foster independence. Beginning the school year by introducing students to two crucial elements of the literacy block—independent reading and independent writing—sets the foundation for a thriving learning environment. By strategically teaching students the different elements of the literacy block, it is possible to develop strong learning routines that continue to evolve and thrive throughout the school year.

What Is AWARD Time?

The thing that separates AWARD Time from other models of literacy instruction is the intentionality with which students' independent work is connected to the learning that is happening during other times during the literacy block. Students take time to work on reading responses directly following guided reading; this allows them time to immediately apply and practice the lessons they have just learned. Similarly, students meet for writing conferences directly after their writing time in order for them to share their work with the teacher and their peers and to receive immediate feedback. As students rotate through the different elements of AWARD Time, they move from guided instruction to independent practice and back to guided instruction in a simple, seamless fashion.

Reading Cycle

Imagine meeting with a group of students for a guided-reading lesson. During this lesson, the students focus on the importance of making connections to their reading. The conversation at the guided-reading table encourages students to share relevant connections and to use this knowledge as a way of enhancing their comprehension of the text. Upon completion of the guided-reading lesson, students return to their desks and apply the lesson they have just participated in. Perhaps they complete a Venn Diagram to identify similarities and differences between the text they have just read and another one, or perhaps they write a reflection about how their personal experiences helped them understand a dilemma that one of the characters they have read about is facing. Whatever the case, they have had an opportunity to meet with the teacher for focused guided instruction followed immediately by an opportunity to apply and practice this learning.

Flash forward to the following day. The group who met with the teacher for guided reading has had an opportunity to practice their new skills in a very scaffolded manner using a text that the teacher has selected. Now, using independent reading books that they have chosen, they have the chance to read independently and apply their learning to a new text, continuing to apply their learning from the previous day to their own texts. For example, one student has selected a simple picture book, another a nonfiction text, and another an online article. These students continue to think about how they can connect to these texts in order to strengthen their comprehension by applying the learning from the previous day to their own self-selected texts. In order to monitor their own learning, the students can complete a simple reading reflection as a way of showing how they were thinking while they were reading.

SAMPLE READING AWARD TIME

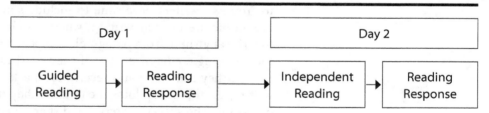

In this simple framework it is easy to see the gradual release of responsibility at work. Students spend time working with the teacher in a focused group to learn a new skill or continue to build on an existing one; this is followed immediately with an opportunity to practice it. The next day, they are able to apply their learning to a new text and continue to expand their learning. When these students return to the teacher for their next guided-reading lesson, the teacher can assess the learning that the students have done based on the way they demonstrated their thinking through the two different reading responses, as well as through the observations and conversations that take place during the guided-reading lesson. Simply put, the teacher is able to triangulate the assessment—using observations, conversations, and products—in order to quickly assess student learning. This opportunity for ongoing assessment and feedback lets the teacher begin each guided-reading lesson with a review/recap of the students' learning from the previous session, assess the students' progress, and use this information as a way of informing further instruction.

Writing Cycle

Students should have frequent ongoing opportunities to meet with the teacher and their peers for feedback. Often, a classroom full of writers is difficult to manage. It is hard to find time to conference with students individually or in small groups to monitor their learning—a real challenge when all students are writing simultaneously. However, if students are writing at different times through the literacy block, then the teacher can strategically plan writing conferences to allow students immediate feedback on their writing. In this manner, students can receive feedback on completed work or work that is in progress; this enables their learning to extend from one writing task to the next.

Imagine another group of learners. This group begins their AWARD Time by working on their independent writing. They select from a range of topics, use writing prompts, or find inspiration in one of many places in the classroom. Perhaps some students are working on new pieces of writing, whereas others are passionately completing pieces from previous writing times. However, there is a common thread between writers. They are using this independent writing time as a way of practicing and "trying-out" the writing that they have been learning with the whole class during Writing Time. Perhaps they are working on narratives or writing for the purpose of persuading. Maybe they are all writing letters to the principal or reports on the latest news events. Regardless of the task, they have had an opportunity for explicit teaching with respect to the form, purpose, and audience for their writing, and are somewhat familiar with the success criteria for it.

After a while, these young writers are anxious to share. In their 15 or 20 minutes, they have had sufficient time to begin their thinking, brainstorm some ideas, and do some writing. Now is the perfect time for the teacher to check in with them. Knowing that the teacher plans to conference with them after 15–20 minutes of writing time gives them a time frame that most writers can adhere to. Younger writers have time to include some words, sentences, and perhaps even a picture in their writing, whereas older writers have had sufficient time to write anywhere from paragraph to a page or two. The students are now ready for a writing conference, even if they don't have a completed piece of writing; in fact, they can share and receive feedback on any piece at any stage in their writing. As this group joins the teacher, they reflect on their goals for this piece of writing (the success criteria) and share their work. They provide and receive feedback from their peers and the teacher. The students then use this feedback to acknowledge their successes, to set and record their personal writing goals, and to identify areas of their writing that might benefit from revision.

Flash forward to the next day. These writers are now ready to continue working on their writing, having had an opportunity to conference with the teacher and their peers. They relish more time to work on their writing, revising their work as suggested or perhaps applying the feedback to a new piece of writing. Again, using independent writing time, they continue to build their writing skills. Finally, anxious to share, these students partner with peers from their group, recalling the conference from the previous day, to revisit personal writing goals and share ways in which they have applied them in their writing.

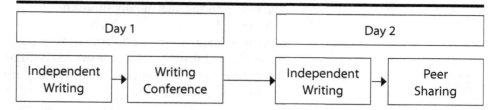

Again, through this simple sequence of tasks, students are able to independently work on their writing, receive immediate feedback, and then apply this feedback to their work.

Why This Instructional Sequence Is So Powerful

Assessment and teaching go hand-in-hand. As you introduce students to new skills, you are constantly monitoring their learning through observations, conversations, and pieces of student work. You can use this ongoing assessment as a way of providing feedback to students and assisting them in setting new goals. Students need to be an active part of the assessment process, identifying their own strengths and setting personal learning goals. When you engage in frequent conversations with learners in guided reading and writing conferences, you are able to listen to students as they talk about their reading, writing, and thinking. You can gain insight into the strategies and processes your students are using and can use this to provide students with immediate feedback and encouragement. When you use AWARD Time as a way of providing focused small-group instruction in tandem with independent, scaffolded practice, you allow students to receive timely, relevant feedback. You are able to teach in a way that responds to individual learning needs and monitor progress as it pertains to each student's strengths and learning goals.

Building AWARD Time

To build strong literacy routines, students need to be able to work independently for sustained periods of time. Initially, this time could be as short as a few minutes, but it can gradually increase until students are able to read or write independently for approximately 15 to 20 minutes. That might not seem like a long time, but these minutes provide the framework upon which the entire literacy block will be built. It is essential that teachers take the time to lay the groundwork for these independent routines. Students need to understand the value of this independent time to both themselves and their peers. It is through independent time that students will practice and apply the skills they are learning throughout the remainder of the literacy block. They will consolidate their thinking and personalize their learning through the choices they make. Establishing the two foundational independent routines of independent reading and independent writing is essential, as it provides opportunities for you to meet with small groups on a daily basis.

Have you ever engaged in a debate with a two-year-old? It is an argument you are certain to lose, or at least surrender and walk away from. When my children were younger, I remember many such conversations. They started innocently with my making a statement, asking a question, or giving an instruction, only to be met with the charmingly innocent response "…but *why*?" Drawn in by their charm and unaware of the direction the conversation was about to take, I would further explain my initial statement. This would lead to the now not-so-charming retort "…but *why*?" The banter would continue for a while until, finally exasperated from the "…but *why*?"s, I would firmly announce, "*Because it just is!*"—thus ending the conversation.

When it comes to establishing strong literacy routines, especially ones that require independence, the "…but *why*?" is essential for youngsters to understand. They need to understand the purpose for their time, the value of the things they are going to be asked to do. They need to know that their work is valid, authentic, and important. They need to understand that it is not just that they are busying themselves so that the teacher can work with other kids, but rather that the work they are doing is helping them become better readers and writers. Their time is being well-spent. Their work is important and they need to use their time wisely. When students understand the *why*, have sufficient choice in their work, and see the purpose for the tasks they are doing, they will likely be more engaged and focused, and better able to remain on-task.

Independent Reading

Imagine buying a new pair of running shoes, putting on a new pair of running shorts, and heading downtown to run your very first marathon on your first-ever day of running. Realistic? Of course not. In the same way, we wouldn't expect our students to return from a summer of playing outside (we'd like to think they spent hours reading, but that's not very likely), flip open a book, and begin to read for a sustained period of time. Just as their muscles need to warm up for running, their brains need time to adjust to the demands of independent reading. For some students, the fact that they are in a classroom again, the excitement that their best friend is in the next desk, and even the whirring noise of the fan are all very real distractions from the books they are trying to read. We need to help them build their stamina slowly, starting with small periods of time and gradually building on their successes until they are able to sustain their reading attention for 15 to 20 minutes.

Initially, students might be able to focus their attention and read independently for only a few minutes. It is better to start with a small goal and celebrate success with your students than to start with an unrealistic goal and face disappointment when they struggle or fail to reach it. You might say something like, "I know we've all been really busy all summer. Do you think we can all read independently for four minutes?" It might seem like a very short time and you may wonder why you should start with such a low target when clearly your students can read for a longer time. But it is better for them to meet with continued success and repeated praise than immediate frustration and possible disappointment. Track your students' accomplishments and every day increase the time they read independently. Each group of students is unique and the rate at which you increase the reading time will vary depending on their specific needs. If the time is increased in two-minute increments each day, within a few weeks students will have reached and exceeded the 15-minute goal.

What do you do with the student who decides to sharpen his pencil during independent-reading time? What about the one who laughs out loud and just

Gail Boushey and Joan Moser (a.k.a. The Sisters) recommend initiating independent reading and writing routines by establishing the purpose and determining the "urgency" of these tasks (2006). They suggest creating I-Charts (Independent Charts) for these routines to help students understand the *why* and *how* of these specific elements. They encourage teachers to brainstorm with their students the reasons for independence, as well as to explicitly model the desired behaviors associated with tasks.

needs to share the funny part of his book with his neighbor? What do we do with someone who absentmindedly flips pages in her book, or the one who never turns a page at all? The burps, the giggles, the coughing fits—they all seem to happen right in the middle of independent reading. When routines are new, some students find it challenging to focus on the task at hand. The awkward silence can be strange for some youngsters, as they sit and wonder what others are reading, thinking, or doing. For some, it is an odd feeling to be reading together and yet independently. For others, reading in their head is a skill they are still trying to master; you might see some youngsters mouthing words as they make sense of the words on the page.

Regardless of the challenges, it is important to constantly remind students of the purpose of this valuable time. Some students might benefit from spending one-on-one time with you, learning how to select books that are a good fit for them, books that they find interesting and can read successfully on their own. For the youngsters who need to share, building in a sharing time immediately following independent reading allows them the opportunity to do just that. The first few days and weeks create the foundations on which the remainder of the literacy block will be built. If students are struggling with these initial routines, you might find it helpful to talk with them privately about the things they are finding challenging about this time. Allow them help from a friend when selecting books, a quiet corner (or place on the carpet) where they can feel more comfortable or less awkward, or a place in the room where they can read aloud in a whisper in order to help make sense of the texts they are reading. By setting realistic class goals, giving lots of positive reinforcement, and addressing the specific needs of the learners, you can encourage all students to strive for independence.

You can't begin to build an independent reading routine without first considering what students are going to read. While helping them select "just right" books is an important skill (and definitely one that needs to be addressed), it might not be essential on the first day. As the literacy routines continue to develop and deepen, there will be plenty of opportunities to provide students with direct instruction on how to select books, abandon books, and so on. However, for the purpose of initiating independent reading, you might allow students time to peruse the classroom library and select a few books that seem interesting to them. While there are many different ways to organize classroom libraries, I have found that using magazine boxes to group books into categories lets students easily locate books of interest to them. Leading up to the launch of your independent-reading routine, provide students with browsing time to select up to six books they can place in a personalized book box; magazine boxes work perfectly for this purpose too, as students can use them to house all of their literacy materials in one place. Encourage each student to choose a range of books (e.g., three picture books, one or two nonfiction texts, and a magazine) and place them in his/her book box. This way, when you are ready to begin the independent-reading routine, students already have a wide selection of books to choose from so that they can read for the required length of time. If you are planning on initiating your independent-reading routine in the first few days of school, consider including an exploration of the classroom library as a "welcome" activity for your new students. It might be a nice way to get to know your youngsters—asking them to share the reasons they were attracted to the books they choose (e.g., Jacob has chosen a nonfiction book about trucks because he likes Mighty Machines; Nayeema has chosen a picture book about Pokemon because she loves to collect cards).

DAY ONE

(Instructional time: approximately 25 minutes)

Begin by gathering the students on the carpet or as a large group at their desks.

Boys and girls, today we are going to start something really important. It is really important because it is something that will help us all learn and work together all year. We are going to start our independent reading today. Think for a moment. Why do you think reading is important?

Allow students a few moments to think about this question.

Perhaps you can tell someone beside you why you think reading is important.

Encourage students to turn to a partner and share their ideas. After students have had an opportunity to talk with a partner, select a few students to share their responses with the whole class. As they share, record their thinking on a chart paper to keep for later reference.

Yes, I agree that reading is very important. In fact, we all learn a lot from reading. We can read nonfiction books to find out information; we can read fiction books to help us imagine new and exciting things; or we could even read a newspaper to find out what is happening in the world. Reading is very important. But how can we learn to be better readers?

Again encourage students to share their ideas with a partner and then with the whole class, recording their ideas on a chart that might look like this one.

SAMPLE CHART: READING

Why is reading important?	What would it look like?
• We learn things from reading.	• We would all have our books and stay in one spot.
• It helps to teach us new words.	• Our eyes would be on the book.
• We can stretch our imagination.	• We would be reading the words with our eyes.
• It helps us find answers to our questions.	

How can we learn to be better readers?	What would it sound like?
• We can learn how to read harder words.	• It would be really quiet.
• We can read faster.	• We would all be reading and thinking in our heads.
• We can practice thinking when we are reading.	
• We can read with more expression.	
• We can work with our teacher and our classmates to practice our reading.	

There are lots of things we can do to become better readers. One really important thing that we need to do is practice reading independently. This means reading on our own. When we are reading independently, we are enjoying our books by ourselves and allowing our friends to enjoy their books by themselves. Reading is hard work and we need make sure that we are thinking while we are reading to make sure that we are understanding the things in the book. We also want to make sure that our friends are able to read their books, so we need to be really quiet so that we can all enjoy our books. What do you think it would look like and sound like in our classroom if everyone were reading their books independently?

Encourage students to share their ideas and then record their suggestions about what it might look like and sound like.

Our brains are a little like our muscles. If we want them to get strong, then we need to exercise them. But when we do exercises, we need to start slowly and gradually do more and more until our muscles are strong. Well, our "reading muscles" are kind of like that. We are going to start building our reading muscles today. We are going to use the books that we have in our book boxes to read independently for four minutes. After four minutes, we are all going to come back together to share some of the things that we have read on our own.

Answer any questions that the students have. Ensure that they are all in appropriate places and have their book boxes (or books) and are ready to begin.

Boys and girls, we are going to read for four minutes starting now.

During this time, stand or sit in a place where you can see the students but are not a focus of their attention. It is not a good idea to wander among the students. The best place to sit would be at the table you will be using for your guided groups, so students will get used to the idea that you are nearby but not hovering.

Once four minutes has elapsed, gently redirect the students, letting them know that their time is up.

You have read independently for four minutes. Please get to a place where you can stop reading—the end of a sentence or paragraph—and be ready to come back together as a class.

If using a carpet, encourage students to return to the carpet and bring the book they have been reading.

I'm sure you all read many interesting or exciting things during this time. Take a few minutes and share with a partner something interesting that you read.

Allow students a few minutes to share their books, talking about a favorite picture, an interesting idea, or the funny part that they just have to share.

How did you feel about reading for four minutes? Do you think that you can read for a little bit longer next time? Tomorrow, our goal will be to read independently for six minutes. For now, please put your books back into your book boxes so that you will have them when you need them again.

Independent Writing

Just as students need to understand the purpose of independent reading, they also need to value their independent-writing time. They will need opportunities to develop their stamina and strengthen their independence when writing on their own. As each student is unique, so too is each class. Only you can decide, using your best judgment, when the time is right to introduce your students to the independent-writing element of the daily literacy block. In some cases, you might choose to introduce students to independent reading and independent writing simultaneously, as both require a similar set of routines and behavioral expectations. Or it might be better to introduce the independent-writing routine once students have had a few days to begin to develop independent-reading routines. Either way, the principles of independent writing are very similar to the ones established for independent reading. To foster independence, you must let students understand the purpose of their work and have the opportunity to gradually increase their stamina when writing. By starting with a very attainable goal, such as writing for four minutes, students can immediately meet with success. It is better to set a target that is easily reached by the entire class than to risk students meeting with frustration or disengagement at the start. Through the process of building this routine, students will begin to write for increasingly longer periods of time, and ultimately be able to sustain their focus when writing for 15 to 20 minutes. By gradually increasing their targets by a minute or two a day, students will increase their stamina when writing.

In the same way that it would be impossible for students to begin independent reading without first having something to read, it is not possible for students to write for sustained periods of time without having something to write about. Prior to initiating the independent-writing routine, encourage students to flip through magazines, newspapers, or flyers and cut out pictures they think are interesting. They can begin to collect these and use them as a source of inspiration when writing. Older students might consider recording interesting newspaper headlines or jotting down story ideas to refer to at later dates. Some students might bring in personal photographs of special places, people, pets, or events they wish to write about. If possible, you might consider creating a classroom Box of Inspiration that could contain images, headlines, story prompts, thought-provoking questions, opinion statements, and anything else that might motivate students to write. Consider creating a chart with the students about some things they might write about. At this early stage in the year, the focus for instruction is more on the routine of writing than on the content of writing. By providing students with the structure of *when* and *why* to write, we will later be able to invest the time in directly supporting them in improving *what* and *how* they write. Regardless of what they are writing, it is much harder for students to develop independent-writing routines if we do not first help them find something to write about.

DAY ONE

(Instructional time: approximately 25 minutes)
Begin by gathering the students on the carpet or as a large group at their desks.

> *Today, we are going to add another really important element to our independent work routines. We are going to begin our independent- writing time. Take a moment to think to yourself:* Why do you think writing is important?

Allow students a few moments to think about this question and share with a partner. Select a few students to share their thinking with the class. As they share, record their thinking on a chart to keep for later reference.

"A successful writing program requires a knowledgeable, organized teacher with excellent classroom management skills. Mostly, students need lots of time in which to write, a say in what they write about, strategies that allow them to problem solve independently (plan, revise, edit), and helpful response."
— Regie Routman (2005)

There are many reasons why writing is important. We can use writing to share our ideas with others or to help us organize our own thinking. Sometimes we write things down so we don't forget something important, and other times we might write so that someone else can learn how to do something new. We might write a story to entertain our friends or a letter to share news with a friend, or we could write a list of things we need to buy at the grocery store. We use writing in lots of different ways and they are all very important.

Now, think about some things that you can do to become a better writer.

Again, allow students an opportunity to share their ideas with their partners and then with the large group. Continue to add their ideas to the chart.

We can all become better writers by practicing our writing, trying to write for different purposes, and sharing our writing with others. Sometimes when our friends read our writing, they are able to give us some ideas that can help us to become better writers. We can learn to use more interesting words and more description in our writing so that the people who read our writing can imagine in their own minds the things we write about.

Finally, think about what it would look like in our class if everyone was writing independently. What would that look like? What would it sound like?

After students share their thinking with their partners, again record their thinking on the chart.

SAMPLE CHART: WRITING

Why is writing important?

- We can share our ideas with others.
- We can write down things that we want to remember.
- Writing can help us organize our ideas.
- We can entertain/persuade/inform others.

How can we learn to be better writers?

- We can learn to use better words.
- We can write for different purposes.
- We can share our writing with our friends and ask for feedback.
- We can set our own writing goals and work toward them.
- We can use a dictionary or thesaurus to check/fix our work.
- We can learn to write more.

What would it look like?

- Everyone would be working at their desk or in a quite spot.
- We would be writing for the whole time.
- Sometimes, we might need to pause and think.

What would it sound like?

- It would be really quiet.
- We would all be thinking and writing on our own.

Do you remember when we said that our brains were a little like our muscles and they needed exercise in order to be able to work for longer periods of time? Well, today we are going to start exercising our "writing muscles." We are going to write independently for four minutes. We will all have an opportunity to share our writing with a friend once the time is over. Before we get started, take a minute to think about something that you'd like to write about.

If the class has previously created a list of potential writing topics, this would be a good time to revisit it or to encourage students to look through the inspiration images/ideas they have started to collect. Start as soon as the students all seem ready to begin and have found a suitable writing place (and have their pencils sharpened).

We are going to write for four minutes starting now.

While students are writing, resist the urge to wander around the classroom. Choose a spot where you are able to observe the students without standing directly over them. Again, the best option would be to sit at the table you are planning on using for small-group instruction. That way, the students become familiar with the routine of working independently while you are working elsewhere in the room.

At the end of four minutes, gently indicate to students that the writing time is now over and they need to return to the carpet or class meeting area.

Boys and girls, you have had an opportunity to write independently for four minutes. Please bring your writing back to our class meeting area. When we write, it's nice to share our writing with our friends. Let's all find a partner and read our writing to them.

Encourage students to partner up and read their own writing to a classmate. Students might need guidance in responding in positive ways and saying only supportive things to each other (e.g., no criticism or put-downs allowed).

How did you feel about writing for four minutes? Do you think that you can write for a little bit longer next time? Tomorrow our goal will be to write independently for six minutes. For now, please put your writing away so you will have it when you need it again.

Congratulations! It may not seem like a significant moment, but you have begun to lay the essential foundational elements for a complete literacy block. When you invest time in establishing routines for independent reading and independent writing, students will understand that the work they do independently is just as important as the work they do when working directly with the teacher. It is through these two independent routines that students will apply, practice, and consolidate the learning that takes place throughout all the other elements of the literacy block. Independent work is not busy-work! It is important time that students can use to work toward their individual learning goals.

Keys to Success: Independent Reading

- Students are able to self-select books.
- Students are able to select an appropriate area to work independently.
- Students understand the purpose and value of reading independently.
- Stamina is built until students can read independently for 15–20 minutes.
- Students are able to independently solve problems that might arise; e.g., solve unfamiliar words without asking, ignore distractions that occur, abandon books when necessary.

- A washroom procedure is established that allows students to go when necessary without needing to ask the teacher; e.g., signing out, putting a washroom pylon on their desk.
- Students have opportunities for sharing periodically.

Keys to Success: Independent Writing

- Students are able to self-select topics or use a class inspiration guide for support.
- Students are able to select an appropriate area to work independently.
- Students understand the purpose and value of writing independently.
- Stamina is built until students can write independently for 15–20 minutes.
- Students are able to independently solve problems that might arise; e.g., spell unknown words without asking, ignore distractions that occur.
- Students can access resources, if necessary, when writing (e.g., dictionary, thesaurus).
- A washroom procedure is established that allows students to go when necessary without needing to ask the teacher; e.g., signing out, putting a washroom pylon on their desk.
- Students have opportunities for sharing periodically.

Day Two and Beyond

On the second day of building the independent routines, begin by reviewing the charts you constructed with the students. You might ask students if they have any additions or changes they would like to make. If you help them understand the purpose of their independent work, students will see it as important, meaningful, and authentic. Students might wish to share some of the things they enjoyed or discovered during their independent work time. For example, some students might want to share something interesting that they read during their reading time, or a writing idea that they were excited to continue working on.

INDEPENDENT READING

Begin by reviewing what happened on Day One:

Yesterday, we started independent reading. This is a very important part of our learning because reading teaches us so many things. Let's review the chart we created yesterday that shows the reasons we think that reading is important and the things we can do to become better readers. Does anyone have anything you think we should add or change on our chart?

Read the chart with the students and add or change ideas as necessary.

We also decided what independent reading should look like and sound like in our classroom. It's really important that we are all working independently. That way, we are all able to do our best work and not interrupt the thinking of our friends.

Review the section of the chart that indicates what independent reading should look and sound like. Add or change as necessary.

When we were reading independently yesterday, did you read anything really interesting that you'd like to share with the class?

Allow a few minutes for peer or whole-class sharing.

Today, our goal will be to read for six minutes. Before we get started, everyone needs to make sure that they have their books at a place in the classroom where you can do your best work. Remember, we will have a chance to share our books with our friends after our reading time, so make sure you don't interrupt anyone during our reading time.

This is a good time to establish washroom routines with students and discuss any other potential challenges they might encounter: e.g., *What should you do if someone beside you is distracting you? What could you do if you are reading and you get to a word you don't know?*
Begin once all students are ready.

We are going to read for six minutes, starting now.

While students are reading, it is best to sit again at the table you are planning on using for small-group instruction. After reading, gather the students at the carpet or class meeting area and encourage them to share something from the books that they read.

Over the next week repeat this procedure. Take a few minutes each day to review the charts, answer questions, and address any challenges that students might be facing. Gradually increase the time the students spend reading independently until they are able to read independently for the desired length of time. This target will vary according to the age of the students and their individual needs; however, 15 to 20 minutes is a reasonable goal.

As students become more comfortable with the routine of reading independently, they need to understand that during this time you will be working with students. At first, the students reading independently might find this distracting; they might pause while reading to observe or listen to the conversation you are having with other students. Over time, students will learn that everyone's work is important, both the work they are doing independently and the work that others might be doing with the teacher.

Boys and girls, you have all been working hard to build up your stamina when reading independently. Today while you are reading, I am going to ask a few people to work with me at our conference table. We will be using whisper-voices so that we don't disturb you. You need to keep doing your work because we all have very important jobs to do. I promise that everyone will have a chance to work with me at the conference table but, when it is not your turn, you need to be working on your independent reading.

You might wish to use this first time to read one-on-one with students, to begin to assess their individual strengths and needs. If you usually complete a diagnostic reading assessment, you might use this time to complete the oral reading portion with students. Continue to reinforce the importance of the work that students are doing, both independently and when working at the conference table with you.

See page 122 for more on forming guided-reading groups.

Once you have completed your initial reading assessments and the students have had sufficient time to develop the routine of independent reading, you are ready to start using this time to conduct guided-reading lessons. You have a good start on observational data, you've had a chance to listen to each child read orally, and you might even have completed a diagnostic reading assessment. Forming guided-reading groups is the next logical step, and now you have a time in your literacy block already designed to accommodate this.

INDEPENDENT WRITING

Use a routine-building process similar to the one used to build the independent-reading routine. Continue to review the charts with students, addressing concerns as they arise and gradually increasing the time that students spend engaged in writing independently. The key to success for building this routine is making sure that students are able to find things that they want to write about. At the start of every independent writing time, allow students to share things they are excited to be writing about or have been writing about. Encourage students to bring in interesting pictures, photographs, and artifacts to contribute to a classroom Box of Inspiration. Record inspiring story ideas, clip interesting newspaper headlines, print pictures of celebrities, and collect creative writing prompts to ensure that students are surrounded by rich writing ideas. Inspiration and engagement are key principles in developing students' independent-writing skills, so invest the time with your students in collecting things that will assist them in making their writing meaningful and purposeful.

In the same way that students need to understand that their independent reading time is also a time that you will use to read with students, they need to understand that their independent-writing time is also a valuable time for you to work with individual students or groups of students. Once students have developed a level of comfort with their daily writing routines, tell them that you will be using this time to conference with individual students about their writing.

Boys and girls, you have all worked hard to develop your independent writing skills. Today, while you are writing, I'm going to ask a few of you to meet me at the conference table. We are going to use this time to talk about a piece of writing that you are the most proud of. I know you have written many things and I want to see your best work. Although I will not meet with everyone today, I promise that everyone will have a chance to meet with me.

Encourage students to take a few moments and flip through their writing books to find the piece of writing they are most proud of. They can mark the page with a sticky note so that they can easily find it when called to the conference table.

Over the next few days, meet briefly with four or five students daily during independent-writing time. You might call together a group of students and encourage them to share their writing with each other or you can meet with students individually.

Keep On Building

These two independent routines are the foundation to the entire literacy block. When you take the time to ensure they are solidly established, everyone greatly benefits for the remainder of the year. Students will use this time to practice and apply the skills they are learning and to set and monitor their personal learning goals.

Periodically throughout the year, it might be necessary to revisit the charts created during the early development of the literacy block. As the year progresses, the literacy block will continue to build. Layer upon layer, students will continue to engage in additional tasks. Regardless of other routines that are added to the literacy block, the foundation remains the same. Solid independent routines provide students with the time necessary to firmly apply and consolidate their learning. In this practice time, students will combine the skills they are actively learning with their personal interests and choices in order to make their learning relevant, authentic, and purposeful.

AWARD Time provides teachers with valuable opportunities to meet with small groups of students and provide immediate feedback on their reading, writing, and thinking. It allows for students to transfer and apply the learning that happens during Reading Time, Writing Time, and small-group instruction. It is based on providing authentic tasks that encourage students to engage in purposeful learning. Providing choice through reading responses, writing ideas, and digital tasks ensures that students have a voice, not only in what they are learning, but also in how they are demonstrating that learning. By introducing each of the AWARD elements through Reading Time and Writing Time, teachers are setting the stage for students to use their time to maximize their learning. Finally, strategically scheduling of the elements of AWARD Time enables students to immediately transfer and apply learning, as they alternate between independent work and small-group guided instruction.

8

Small-Group Learning

Small-group instruction is the vehicle through which teachers are able to monitor individual students and provide them with differentiated instruction based on their strengths and needs. By meeting with students regularly, we are able to determine which areas are their strengths and to pinpoint areas for further instruction. Small groups allow time for students to share their learning with their peers and to give and receive feedback with each other. They can use this time to set individual learning goals and monitor their progress in achieving the goals they have previously set. From an assessment perspective, small groups give you a practical way of regularly assessing students and using these observations to guide instruction, form new groups, and individually tailor instructions to better suit the needs of each learner.

Small-group instruction provides a safe place for students to engage in rich conversations about texts, their work, and their thinking. Through these dialogues, they are able to articulate their thinking, justify their ideas, even question and build on the ideas of their peers. This rich, accountable talk provides opportunities for students to expand their thinking about their reading and writing. In these focused group settings, students are able to share their work with each other in a way that is risk-free and respectful. They are able to provide feedback to their peers, as well as receive feedback from their teacher. It is this instantaneous cycle of learning, sharing, and feedback that has the most direct impact on student achievement.

Students are able to use the vehicle of talk to share their thoughts about texts without being restricted by their writing abilities. In this way, the teacher is able to combine students' conversations with observations made during guided instruction and with the products students create during independent-work time to form a complete profile of each learner. This triangulation of assessment is important when assessing students' understanding and thinking, especially as it relates to reading. Often students' reading ability is assessed solely on their ability to write. Although this reading–writing connection is significant, it should not be the only means of judging a student's thinking in response to written texts. According to Reggie Routman (2003):

> We can make the most of our reading time with students by making it a richer instructional context: demonstrating a new literacy form, connecting it to the curriculum and inviting active participation. In particular, the opportunities for talk about the texts are critical.

Similarly, providing students with immediate feedback on their written work allows students to continue and extend their learning. Meeting with students frequently for writing conferences lets the teacher constantly monitor and assess each student's learning in relation to specific learning goals. When provided with opportunities to talk about their writing with their peers, students are able to share feedback with each other and consider all sources of feedback (peer and teacher) when reflecting on their work and setting personal learning goals. Often when students share their writing aloud, they are able to reflect more accurately on their work; this gives them a chance to expand their ideas and respond to the questions of their peers. As authors they are able to share their writing with expression, enabling their peers and teacher to "hear" the piece as the author intended.

Forming Instructional Groups

Initially, it is tempting to place students into learning groups based on their individual reading abilities and the levels at which they are reading. In the lower grades, this is probably the easiest and most practical way of grouping students. Guided-reading resources are often designed to differentiate by reading level and provide a good starting point for grouping students. After initial assessments you might be able to form groups of students based on the level of texts that they are able to read with accuracy.

However, there are other ways of grouping students. What if students were grouped according to their personal interests? The teacher would be able to select texts for guided-reading times that reflect the specific interests of the students within the group. For example, some students become very excited at the idea of reading nonfiction information about snakes, whereas others are repulsed. Some students eagerly read fiction stories about magic, whereas their counterparts find this kind of text disturbing. If students' choices are reflected in the books they are asked to read, no doubt their motivation and engagement will be heightened.

Another possibility when grouping students is to carefully analyze each students' current areas of strength and areas of need. For example, some students make substitution errors while reading, some lack fluency and expression or ignore punctuation when they read, whereas others decode beautifully but lack comprehension of the material they are reading. By grouping students according to their specific instructional needs, the teacher can spend time explicitly addressing these needs with each group of students. It is also helpful for students to engage in conversations with their peers, realizing that everyone is working on strengthening their skills but in different areas.

So at times we might choose to place students together who are working at similar instructional levels. But we should remain cautious about always grouping students in this manner. If we want our struggling readers to benefit from the ideas of others, they need to have opportunities to share their thinking with students of different abilities. If we want to ensure that our students are engaged, at times student grouping needs to reflect the interests of the students. Also, there may be times when students at different instructional levels are all working on similar individual learning goals and can be placed into groups according to these personal learning goals. Flexible groupings allow students to work collaboratively with different students and not feel that the grouping is a reflection of where they fit in the hierarchy of abilities in the classroom. Learning groups allow you to provide direct instruction to individual students in focused areas of learning. By strategically grouping students, you are able to maximize this instruction and provide opportunities for students to learn from and with each other.

As groups are initiated, it is important to impress upon students that these groups are not "forever" groups. Once literacy routines are established, frequently revisit student groupings and re-group students as necessary. As students learn things and different skills become the instructional focus throughout the year, the way you group students should reflect the changing dynamics of the class-room. On average, student groupings should change monthly; sometimes they need to change more frequently. It is through these short, focused, explicit teaching opportunities that students make the most rapid development as learners. By regularly assessing their progress and re-evaluating their needs, you ensure that the time spent in guided-reading groups is most valuable.

A Group by Any Other Name

Like it or not, labels are important. When forming groups, consider using creative group names rather than color names or numbers (e.g., the Red group, or Group #1). If groups are numbered, students might equate these numbers with ability levels or even rankings. If you use a set of names that follow a class theme or mimic the school team identity, students will take greater pride in their association with their group; for example, teams named after popular sports teams, mythical creatures, types of storms, animals, planets, etc. Of course, ensure that all group names have a positive connotation and cannot be interpreted in a negative fashion; e.g., naming a group the Turtles implies that they are slow. As groups change, students can be involved in selecting new names for the groups or group names might reflect a current classroom theme.

Guided Reading

"The aim of guided reading is to develop independent readers who question, consider alternatives and make informed choices as they seek meaning. Guided reading is an enabling and empowering approach where the focus is on the child as a long-term learner being shown how and why and which strategies to select and employ to ensure that meaning is gained and maintained during reading and beyond." — Mooney (1990)

Small-group instruction is the time when teachers are able to interact on a personal level with students about texts. Teacher and students can read together, think together, and share their ideas while interacting with the text. Teachers can monitor students' progress and use this ongoing assessment to inform their instruction.

A typical guided-reading lesson ranges from 15 to 20 minutes in length. Ensure that students are spending the majority of this time reading the text. The lessons should provide an opportunity for you to set the stage for reading, to engage students in thoughtful discussions during reading, and to allow for reflection after reading. Although it is important to plan guided-reading lessons in advance, it is essential that the lesson be flexible enough to allow you to modify as needed. When you observe students reading and engaging in conversations, you will be able to monitor the students' learning and adjust the instruction as needed.

The goal of guided instruction is to equip students with skills and strategies they will transfer into their independent reading. It is a crucial link in the sequence of the gradual release of responsibility. Teachers are able to use this guided time as a way to monitor and support each student in their learning. Guided-reading lessons should enable students to make explicit connections between the skills they are learning with the teacher and the ones that they are practicing on their own. According to Richard Allington (2002),

> Expert teaching requires knowing not only how to teach strategies explicitly, but also how to foster transfer of the strategies from the structured practice activities to students' independent use of them while engaged in reading.

Explicitly linking students' independent work with the skills they are learning through guided lessons enables them to directly transfer their learning.

A typical guided-reading lesson can be organized into three instructional components: before reading, during reading, and after reading.

Before Reading

Before reading, set the context for reading. Helping students activate prior knowledge and make initial predictions will help them begin to engage with the text.

- When introducing a text, encourage students think about the title and the cover in order to make some initial predictions.
- Students can take an initial flip-through of the text, examining the pictures, images, headings, captions, or other text features that help them begin to make meaning from the text.
- Introduce the purpose for the guided-reading lesson by explicitly stating the skills that will be the focus of the lesson, as well as why and how this will help students as readers.
- Introduce or review specific reading strategies that will be the focus of the lesson.
- You might start by providing some background information on the text: e.g., stating whether it is fiction or nonfiction, sharing how it is connected to other areas of classroom learning.
- Introduce the ways in which students might be asked to share their thinking/ responding with their peers: e.g., use sticky notes to mark important ideas, record questions on a chart, compare ideas using a Venn diagram.

During Reading

While students are reading, introduce students to new and interesting vocabulary that they will encounter. Pause to pose questions and reflect on important ideas throughout the text.

- Try to keep discussions focused on one reading skill or strategy and the ways in which students are able to apply this to the text.
- Instruction should be focused and yet also flexible, so it can be adapted to best suit students' specific learning needs.
- Students should be given an opportunity to pre-read a section of text before they are asked to read it to the group (as opposed to round-robin reading, in which students take turns to read different sections of the text).
- Encourage students to identify passages of text they would be willing to share aloud that support their thinking.
- Chunk the text into manageable pieces (e.g., a paragraph, a page) and allow students time to read it in their heads or using a whisper-voice.

After Reading

In a recent study, Wood (2006) found a significant correlation between oral reading fluency and reading comprehension.

After reading a text, students should have an opportunity to reflect on the text as a whole. They might need to revisit the initial introduction of the lesson, thinking about which skills or strategies they were using most while reading.

- You might revisit questions posed before and during reading the text and allow students to engage in a discussion about their thinking.
- Encourage students to respond to questions that promote higher-order thinking by justifying their opinions with evidence from the text.
- Ask students to reflect on the specific reading strategy or skill that was the focus of the lesson and think about how it helped them better understand the text.
- Provide students with feedback based on your observations and conversations throughout the guided-reading lesson. These comments should be positive and encouraging, enabling students to continue to set and reflect on their personal learning goals.
- Consider ways in which students can transfer and apply the learning to their independent reading or other contexts.
- Provide engaging activities that help strengthen students' understanding of the text: e.g., create a chart, write a letter to the author.
- Use observational and conversational data to inform decisions for further instruction for each student.
- You might find it helpful to record observations on a class tracking sheet; recording students' personal learning goals will assist when you plan future lessons or adjust groupings.

Guiding Questions

The charts on pages 130–134 focus on specific reading strategies and provide questions teachers and students might find helpful. While these questions can be used as a starting point, teachers are encouraged to formulate questions that are personalized to each group of students and relate specifically to each text being read.

Writing Conferences

Writing conferences allow time for small groups of students to share their writing and provide feedback to each other. The teacher is able to use this time for focused guided instruction and individualized goal-setting for each student. As students share their writing, the teacher is able to monitor each student's learning, provide immediate feedback, and assist the student in setting realistic goals for continued learning.

When students are writing, a well thought-out sequence of routines can turn writing busy-work into intentionally structured times to try out writing skills, set personal writing goals, and apply feedback. If the teacher plans to meet with two groups of students a day (once for guided reading and once for a writing conference), then strategic planning can help make the most of these instructional times. If some students use independent-work time to work on their writing, then this time should be immediately followed by a writing conference with the

A final element to complete the writing cycle would be a time for students to practice their word skills, practicing words they are authentically using in their independent writing. See page 129 for more on word skills.

teacher. How beneficial would it be for students to meet with their teacher and receive immediate feedback on the writing they have just done?

In this cycle, students use their independent writing time to write for 15 to 20 minutes; during the second portion of AWARD Time, they can conference with the teacher and receive immediate feedback. In the same way that the reading cycle relies on the gradual release of responsibility, so does the writing cycle. On the second day of the writing cycle, students can begin by applying the feedback from the writing conference to revise or continue their work during independent writing.

Feedback

Feedback is most helpful when it is descriptive and skill-based, rather than motivational, in nature. For example, feedback like "Great work!" or "This is amazing!" might encourage learners but it doesn't give any guidance as to how they can improve their work. Imposing personal judgment on a student's learning with comments like "I'm proud of you" implies that a student should be motivated by external forces, such as pleasing the teacher or getting a good mark. Feedback is most effective when it encourages students to reflect on their previous goals and measure their work in relation to them. Feedback that is evaluative in nature, like "This is Level 3 work," can give students some indication as to the level of their success but fails to help students determine areas for continued growth and development with their learning. Effective descriptive feedback should assist students in reflecting on their work, identifying their areas of strength, and setting learning goals for continued improvement.

Lorna Earle (2003) states, "It isn't enough for teachers to see the next steps and use them in their planning. Students need to see them as well." As teachers we recognize the importance of using assessment as a tool to guide our instruction; however, students are an integral component of this assessment process and they need ongoing feedback about their progress. In order for feedback to be the most effective part of assessment it needs to assist students in determining where they are in relation to the success criteria and what their next step should be.

During a writing conference the teacher and students might find it helpful to refer to mentor texts as well as the success criteria. Doing this, they can consider ways in which the success criteria are demonstrated in authentic writing situations. Effective feedback needs to contain information that students will find useful and easy to apply. If students have previously engaged in determining success criteria, they can then measure their progress in relation to these learning targets. Shirley Clarke (2001) encourages teachers to set clear learning targets with students and to display them prominently in the classroom. By revising them frequently, we ensure that they remain the fundamental focus for learning. When we provide feedback, we are providing students with an understanding of where they are in relation to the target. We are able to help them identify which success criteria they were able to demonstrate in their writing and what would be the next logical step for them in order to continue to work toward their goal.

According to Susan Brookhart (2008), "Effective feedback describes the student's work, comments on the process the student used to do the work, and makes specific suggestions for what to do next." Based on her work, the following suggestions might help you provide effective feedback to students:

- **Feedback needs to be timely.** We need to provide students with feedback about their learning while the student is still thinking about the learning.
- **Feedback needs to be purposeful.** Feedback provided to students needs to be skill-specific rather than task-specific. Provide students with feedback about the things they will continue to have the opportunity to practice.
- **Limit the amount of feedback.** Don't try to correct everything; instead, provide feedback about the most important, relevant, and useful areas.
- **Relate the feedback to the goal.** Describe students' learning in terms of the success criteria and assist them in setting goals that will move them closer to their target.
- **Feedback should be free of judgment.** Feedback should describe students' learning and assist them in setting targets, rather than having the purpose of assigning a mark or imposing personal judgment on the students' work or effort.
- **Feedback should be in relation to a continuum of learning.** Identify ways in which students' work has improved and assist them in setting one or two goals that are attainable for next time.
- **Feedback needs to demonstrate a tone of respect.** Use a tone that demonstrates your recognition that the students are in control of their writing and their learning.
- **Feedback should encourage reflection.** Try to pose questions that cause the students to become reflective of their work in relation to the success criteria.

A writing conference is not a time when students hand their work over to the teacher in order to have it corrected. Often teachers believe that fixing a student's work benefits the student in some way. Some writing conferences include lines of students waiting for the teacher to edit their writing so that they can then re-copy it as a final copy.

As a writer myself, I can tell you that the most effective learning that I have done through the writing process has been through receiving queries from my editor. When a true editor reads a manuscript or document, their role is not to fix the mistakes but to draw the author's attention to areas of confusion and areas that need improvement, by posing questions in a way that cause the author to revise and rework the piece. It is not until a text is complete that the editor will fix the mistakes in order to get it ready for publishing. At that time, the author is well-removed from the text and need only review the document one final time. It is the querying stage of the writing process that engages the author in the reflective process. This is the most powerful part of learning. This is what we need to capture and bring into our classrooms.

When we ask our students to reflect on their writing by posing thoughtful questions, we enable them to be an active part of the process rather than a passive observer. When the teacher corrects a student's writing, the student is no longer in control of the work. The student has handed it over to someone else to fix and therefore is no longer responsible for the piece. All too often, teachers get frustrated with students because they seem to continually make the same mistakes and don't transfer the corrections from one writing piece to another. If a student is not an active part of the process when the corrections are made, they are not actively learning; therefore, it is not realistic to expect the students to transfer understanding to a new situation. The student must remain in control of his or her writing and be responsible for rethinking and revising it as necessary. Descriptive feedback allows the students to see their writing from a critical standpoint and reflect on their learning. If they are encouraged to set goals for further learning, rather than focusing on fixing errors, they will be able to apply this learning to subsequent pieces of writing.

Writing conferences should always focus on the learner and the learning rather than just the specific piece. Teachers need to tailor feedback to meet each student's individual learning needs. A student's learning does not occur in isolated chunks; instead, each assignment continues to build the student's repertoire of skills. As students continue along this journey, we can use their previous work as a measure for their new learning. They should be encouraged to reflect on the learning that has already taken place in order to set the stage for continued growth.

Engaging All Authors

Sitting at a conference table and listening to their peers share their writing can be tedious for students. Some students find this process interesting; however, in all likelihood, they will consider this a time of waiting for their turn to share. For example, if a teacher meets with a group of five students for a writing conference, it might seem possible to listen attentively to only one student at a time. In that time, what are the other four students doing? Are they patiently waiting their turn? Are they asked to listen quietly to each student's writing? Or is it possible to include them in the discussion and feedback process? Is it possible to engage all of the students around the table? How can we teach students to provide effective descriptive feedback to each other and maximize the learning that is taking place during writing conferences?

Involving all students in rich conversations about each piece of writing allows students to share the role of expert. Students need to be able to share feedback with their peers in supportive, respectful ways. The feedback prompts on page 135 might be helpful when you are asking students to provide feedback to each other.

Another strategy you might find helpful when trying to engage all students during a writing conference is to assign each a specific role during the conference. For example, if students are learning how to write persuasive pieces, each student could be assigned a specific element of the success criteria to listen for. The Main Idea Monitor could listen carefully to ensure that the writer has clearly stated the main idea; the Fact Finder could listen to determine whether or not the writer has provided sufficient information to justify or prove his/her point of view; a Conclusion Captain could listen to make sure that the piece has a clearly stated conclusion; and the Editor could keep an eye out for appropriate use of conventions. These roles could rotate as students share their work. Using this strategy, students are all active participants in the sharing and reflecting process. They are all responsible for listening actively and providing feedback to their peers. They not only are learning by sharing their own writing and receiving feedback, but are also able to learn from their peers. They can observe how others are working toward the success criteria and how they are setting and monitoring personal goals, and they can actively provide thoughtful feedback by posing reflective questions or sharing observations with their peers. In this way, the writing conference becomes a valuable time of sharing, reflecting, and learning for all participants.

Tracking Student Goals

In a classroom of students, it becomes a significant challenge for a teacher to track and monitor each student's individual learning goals. We need to develop strategies that allow us to easily record and revisit students' successes as well as to keep track of their learning goals. You might find it helpful to keep a clipboard handy and take a few moments after each writing conference to record observations about a student's learning, recording a significant strength that the student demonstrated in writing or noting the goal the student set for him/herself.

But if we want our students to be active participants in the assessment and learning processes, we need to make sure they are able to reflect on the feedback that is provided in the writing conference. A simple but effective tracking strategy is for students to record a personal writing goal on the top of the next page in their writing book. The next time students sit to write, they will be able to focus their attention on meeting that goal. It becomes a simple way for students to share the goals they are working on with their peers, as well as to monitor their goals over time. Flipping through a student's writing book, a teacher can clearly see which goals the student has been working on, how long the student has worked on specific goals, and how that student has applied these goals in his/her writing. Students' writing books contain a regular log of their goals and evidence of how they have progressed as writers. This is a valuable tool for students to use when reflecting on their learning over time, as well as clear evidence for a teacher to share with parents or guardians when discussing a student's progress. With this simple tracking tool, parents and guardians are able to share in a student's learning and support their child as he/she sets and works toward new goals.

"With the time pressures common in today's classroom, it is tempting to assign exercises from a speller as homework and simply dictate words at the end of the week. However, unless the concepts are linked in weekly units to everyday writing and other word-study activities, the age-old problem of transferring work knowledge to writing is likely to continue. A Friday dictation should not be a measure of success of a student's spelling." —Scott & Siamon (2004)

Embedding Word Skills

As students are engaging in authentic writing situations, it becomes possible for the teacher to monitor their understanding of word skills. While many teachers have moved away from traditional spelling textbooks or weekly spelling lists, word skills remain an important aspect of regular literacy instruction. The hot debate about whether or not to teach spelling has resulted in many teachers being unsure about how to effectively develop proficiency with this skill. Weekly spelling lists don't provide the differentiation and personalization necessary for students to transfer their learning to their writing; however, there remains a need to actively teach word skills, word meanings, and various word patterns.

A writing conference is a perfect time for teachers to observe how students are using their word skills in authentic writing situations. Together, teacher and students can engage in conversations about frequent word usage, determining which words or word skills need to be a focus for continued learning. For example, a teacher observes that one student is unsure about how to write verbs in the past tense (e.g., regular verbs: *walked, played*; and irregular verbs: *ran* instead of *runned, ate* instead of *eated*); another student has frequent substitutions due to word-usage errors (e.g., *there/their/they're*); and another needs to strengthen his repertoire of frequently used words (*because, said, went*, etc.).

When word skills are embedded into authentic learning situations, students will be more likely to transfer their use to new writing situations. A writing conference is a time when the student can receive focused individualized guidance in order to strengthen writing skills in all areas.

Questions for Guided Reading

Visualizing
Using all of our senses to create mental images as we read

Guiding Questions

Before
- Which senses can you use when visualizing a text?
- How does visualizing help you to understand a text?

During
- Which senses you are using to visualize the text?
- Are there key words the author uses to help you determine which senses you should be using? (e.g., "odor," "fragrance," "stench," etc. are connected to sense of smell)

After
- Which words/phrases/passages helped you visualize the text?

Learning Goals
- Use mental images to strengthen comprehension of text.
- Identify key words/phrases that help the reader to visualize.
- Explain how the reader can use each of the senses to visualize and interpret the text.

Determining Importance
Deciding what information is important and relevant

Guiding Questions

Before
- What do you think will be the big idea of the text?
- Why do you think the author wrote this text? What does he/she want you to know?

During
- How can you tell the difference between ideas that are interesting and ideas that are important?
- How does the author draw your attention to specific information he/she wants you to notice?

After
- Which ideas do you think were the most important? How did the author make that clear to the reader?
- What is the main idea of the text? What information/details support it?

Learning Goals
- Determine the main idea of a text and provide supporting details.
- Distinguish between ideas that are important and relevant and ideas that are interesting but irrelevant.
- Use text features to identify the author's key messages.

Pembroke Publishers © 2012 *100 Minutes* by Lisa Donohue ISBN 978-1-55138-276-0

Questions for Guided Reading, cont'd

Questioning
Asking questions as we read to help us engage with the text and monitor our understanding

Guiding Questions

Before
- When you flip through this text, what are you wondering about?
- What are some questions you have about the text?

During
- What questions can you ask yourself to make sure that you understand the text?
- What questions do you have as you are reading?
- Are there things that you find confusing?

After
- Were you confused about anything in the text?
- Do you have any questions that are still unanswered?
- What is something that you would have liked to ask the author/characters?

Learning Goals
- Ask questions to help strengthen comprehension of the text.
- Use questioning to help identify and remember important information in the text.
- Ask a variety of "thick" questions (*why, what if*) and "thin" questions (*who, where, when*).
- Generate questions that could lead to further inquiry.

Connecting
Making meaningful connections to the text to strengthen comprehension

Guiding Questions

Before
- Do you recognize anything familiar in this text?
- Do any of the pictures/titles/headings remind you of anything?

During
- Where have you seen/heard this before?
- Do any of the characters in the story remind you of anyone you know?
- Is there information in the text that is different from what you originally thought?

After
- In which way does this text remind you of another text?
- Have you ever had a similar experience?

Learning Goals
- Use personal experiences, other texts, or knowledge of the world to extend the meaning of the text by connecting to the subject, theme, characters, setting, or plot.

Pembroke Publishers © 2012 *100 Minutes* by Lisa Donohue ISBN 978-1-55138-276-0

Questions for Guided Reading, cont'd

Inferring
Using information in the text to form ideas or conclusions that are implied but not directly stated

Guiding Questions

Before
- What do you think might be the purpose of the text?
- What message do you think the author might have been trying to send the reader?
- Based on clues you get from the cover (or by flipping through the text), what do you think the text will be about? What do you think you will learn by reading this text? What do you think will be the big idea of the text?

During
- Are there clues that are helping you make a prediction about what might happen next?
- How can you determine how a character (or the author) feels about the events/topic?
- Who is telling the story? How do you know that you are hearing his/her point of view?

After
- Which clues in the text did you think were the most important?
- What conclusions did you make about the text? What evidence did you use to come to these conclusions?
- What was the big idea that the author wanted to express? What elements in the story combined to help tell that message?
- If you could hear someone else's side of the story, whose would it be, and what do you think they might say?

Learning Goals
- Combine clues from the text with personal experiences or prior knowledge to form conclusions about the text.
- Think beyond the literal meaning of texts and make predictions, conclusions, or judgments about what the author may have implied.

Pembroke Publishers © 2012 *100 Minutes* by Lisa Donohue ISBN 978-1-55138-276-0

Questions for Guided Reading, cont'd

Synthesizing
Combining new information with existing knowledge to form a new opinion or idea

Guiding Questions

Before
- What do you already know about this subject?
- What are your opinions or thoughts about this topic?
- How do you think the author feels about this subject? How might he/she try to convince you to agree with this?

During
- What prior knowledge and experiences are you using to help you interpret the text?
- How does the author's perspective compare to your personal experiences/prior knowledge?
- What information in the text do you think will be the most important at the end?

After
- How did your previous experiences/knowledge compare to the information in the text?
- Did your opinion on the subject change at all? If so, what did the author say that helped to change your opinion?

Learning Goals
- Use information from texts and your own ideas to form conclusions, judgments, or new opinions.
- Use a variety of sources to collect information on a subject and to create a broader understanding of the topic at hand.

Pembroke Publishers © 2012 *100 Minutes* by Lisa Donohue ISBN 978-1-55138-276-0

Questions for Guided Reading, cont'd

HOT
Using higher-order thinking to evaluate the text and make judgments and conclusions about it

Guiding Questions

Before
- What do you think is the purpose of the text?
- What was the intended audience for the text? What makes you think that?
- How does the author attempt to capture the reader's attention?

During
- Which parts of the text do you think work well in expressing the author's purpose?
- How do you know who the intended audience for the text is?
- Is there anything you notice that might be missing from the text?
- Do you agree with the information/ideas being presented?

After
- Which parts of the text do you think were the most effective in expressing the author's message?
- What ideas do you agree or disagree with? Why do you feel that way?
- Is there another perspective you would like to hear on the subject?

Learning Goals
- Use information in the text and your own ideas to make judgments and conclusions about the text.
- Evaluate the text in order to determine the accuracy and validity of the source and content.
- Think critically about the content of texts.

Pembroke Publishers © 2012 *100 Minutes* by Lisa Donohue ISBN 978-1-55138-276-0

Feedback Prompts for Writing Conferences

- What was your goal? How did you work toward your goal?

- What did you want your audience to notice?

- I noticed…

- I was confused about…

- The part I connected to the most was…

- I was able to visualize the part where…

- The part that worked well was…

- Your writer's voice was strongest when…

- What did you do well that created the results you wanted?

- Did you consider…?

- You really showed your learning by…

- Is this something you're planning to continue working on?

- What was your focus for writing?

- After writing, which part were you the most proud of?

- What did you learn or try in this piece that you'll try again next time?

PART FIVE

Maintaining the Balance

Derek huddles in a corner, thumbing through a nonfiction book filled with weird but true facts. His mind races as he pores over the information.

Wow, it's possible to use elephant dung to make electricity. How do they get the electricity out? How did they discover this? he wonders.

If a major-league baseball is used for an average of six pitches, I wonder what a typical nine-inning game costs in baseballs alone? he ponders.

If some frogs freeze almost solid in the winter, what happens when they start to thaw out? Do they just come back to life? Does it happen all at once, or slowly?

As he continues to read, his mind is filled with questions—questions he will need to resolve. Questions that have made him pause, wonder, question, and think. How can he begin to find the answers?

Wonderful! he thinks…and the doors to inquiry have opened.

Derek heads to the counter and picks up a handheld device. Within minutes he is searching for answers to his burning questions. He knows how to explore and examine the information he finds. He has been taught how to evaluate websites for accuracy and reliability. He thinks critically and analytically about the information he encounters. His learning has meaning, significance, and relevance. He is completely engaged and actively exploring through inquiry. With the tasks seamlessly integrated into his reading time, Derek has read a variety of texts, questioned, explored, thought, and responded. This is independence in action: using reading as a catalyst for inquiry; using inquiry as a basis for exploration.

Meanwhile, Indigo is putting the final touches on her letter to a popular snack-food provider. In science she has been exploring various packaging materials and their long-term effect on the environment. She has researched different options and is more than eager to share her opinions with the people who make the decisions. She is convinced that her information is important and that it will challenge the company's existing practice.

Indigo's letter is formal and filled with relevant information. She has collected information from a variety of sources and organized it in a way she feels will best convey her idea. During her independent-reading time, Indigo has chosen to use online sources and nonfiction books to help build her argument; she uses her writing time to craft a powerful letter based on her findings. Her reading and writing are connected in authentic ways that allow her to write for a purpose and to a real audience.

She eagerly seeks input from her friends, asking for feedback about whether her opinion is stated clearly but not aggressively. She asks if her background information is accurate and concise enough to support her suggestions. She wonders if she should address the information she found that counters her argument or if she should just ignore it. These are questions that guide her thinking and help shape her writing; questions that are important and relevant; questions that can be answered only through collaboration with a community of writers. Indigo eagerly shares with her friends, seeking input from people whose opinions she respects, values, and appreciates. This is collaboration in action: a writing community where writing takes shape through ongoing sharing and feedback.

9

Building In New Literacies

Integrating Digital Technology and Media Literacy

Technology in the classroom should not be considered an add-on. It should not be a separate component of the literacy program, standing in isolation of all of the other learning that is happening. It should support and expand students' learning and directly connect to the content and skills that are being taught during other instructional times.

The use of digital tools—computers, laptops, netbooks, and tablets—and the BYOD (Bring Your Own Device) movement have made it possible to connect our students to the world. We are able to remove our classroom boundaries and connect, collaborate, and create with others beyond our school, city, or even country. The portability and accessibility of digital tools is making it more and more possible for teachers to integrate current real-time events into classroom experiences. Digital tools are not a new element in teaching; in reality, they are no longer even considered optional. We need to use these tools as a way of teaching our students how to interpret material that they find online, how to create and share content in responsible ways. We need to teach them responsible digital citizenship and how to be critically literate of the information they encounter. We need to help them learn cyber-safety and teach them how to locate, evaluate, and analyze online information. By integrating digital tools into our classrooms, we allow our students to apply their reading, writing, speaking, and listening skills in authentic learning situations. These tools are valuable when we teach students to connect, communicate, create, collaborate, consolidate, and critically analyze. The integration of digital tools into the classroom helps students become more globally aware, more proactive, and more engaged.

How Young Is Too Young?
— Angie Harrison (Kindergarten Teacher)

The students entering our Kindergarten classrooms are children whose lives have already been immersed in technology. A walk through a mall or a hockey arena will yield a panorama of very young children holding their parents' cell phones, borrowing their tablets, or using their own iPods. As students enter school, educators can help them understand what powerful tools these devices are for learning. Children need to be guided and supported so they understand that digital devices can be used as tools to help consolidate their thinking and learning, as well as to help communicate their ideas. It is important that we support parents in developing their understanding of how computers, tablets, cell phones, and other

---

devices can support learning. Teachers can engage parents in this process by using these tools to document and share the learning occurring in the classroom, and to connect it with learning that can occur at home. Digital photos e-mailed to work, e-books sent home, a Skype hello in the middle of the day, and digital drawings uploaded to blogs are ways to connect with parents. The devices are already in their lives; it's our moral imperative to guide learners in being responsible digital citizens as soon as they enter our school buildings.

The Six Cs of Digital Literacy

For more on the six Cs, see *Keepin' It Real* (Donohue, 2010).

With the integration of digital tools, students can use the six *C*s of digital literacy to extend and expand on the learning that is happening in their classroom.

1. Connect: Digital tools allow students to connect with the world without leaving the classroom. They can go on virtual field trips or examine images from other parts of the world. They can read, listen, watch, and experience the things that happen outside the walls of their school. Students can research world events in real time. With digital tools, students no longer need to be passive observers of the world around them. They are able to connect with the world, communicate with others, and add their voices to issues as they happen.

2. Communicate: When we communicate with others, we are able to gather and share information. Communication in the 21st century seamlessly flows between face-to-face interactions and online communications. Through the use of digital tools in the classroom—blogs, class websites (such as Moodle or Edmodo), even Twitter—students are able to learn how to communicate in an online environment. While the digital world may seem a scary place for many educators, there are numerous tools that are secure; only students and the teacher are able to access the site and the information contained therein. Within these platforms, students can share their work, collaborate with others, and provide feedback to their peers using a wide variety of media.

Screenshot reproduced with permission from Edmodo, http://ge.tt/7VmyOhK?c#!/7VmyOhK

Digital Tools for Communication

www.edmodo.com   Edmodo is a secure platform that allows students to share information, post links to other sites, and upload work from other media sites. Through Edmodo, it is possible for teachers to form small groups, connect with students in other classes or schools, and ultimately collaborate in a secure online environment.

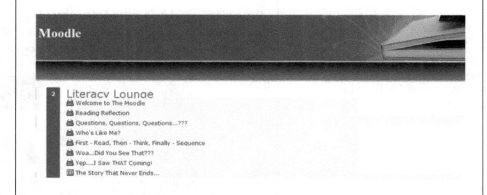

www.moodle.org Moodle is an online classroom management system. It is a place where teachers can create and post assignments, and share links to other sites. With a Moodle, students can share their assignments with the teacher or peers in a safe, secure setting. Teachers can provide feedback as well as monitor students' usage while they are online. Within a Moodle, it is possible to create a wide range of assignments including forums (similar to blog posts), journals (accessible only by the teacher), chats (instant messaging, archived for teachers to access at a later date), tests, quizzes, and much more.

3. Create: Creativity is directly linked to inspiration, and inspiration is connected to engagement. When tasks are creative and engaging, students are more motivated. Students can use digital tools in new and innovative ways to share and reflect on their learning. Through the use of digital tools, students can synthesize and integrate their learning in creative ways.

Digital Tools for Creating

These are just a couple of simple tools students can use to create different media works as an integrated way of reflecting on their learning. While there are hundreds of accessible resources, perhaps the ones shared here will help spark your imagination and serve as a starting point.

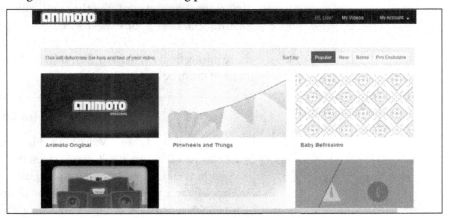

www.animoto.com   Animoto is a user-friendly tool that allows students to upload images and videos to create a dynamic slideshow. Users are able to add music and text to produce one-of-a-kind video presentations. When completed, these videos can be downloaded or shared by posting a link to the video. Users create an online account that allows them to store all their videos in the cloud, from which they can be accessed from any online device.

www.bighugelabs.com   Big Huge Labs is an online tool that allows users to create a variety of media images (including motivational posters, magazine covers, movie posters, and more). Students can simply upload images and add text to create vivid, professional-looking products. Think of the possibilities when asking students to respond to reading, promote their writing, or reflect on their learning!

4. Collaborate: With digital tools, students are able to collaborate in new and innovative ways. Within many classes students can collaborate face-to-face or use digital tools as a way of meeting and collaborating with others. Some tools allow for multiple users; for example, Google Apps allows students to work on collaborative tasks simultaneously. Other tools provide the opportunity for students to share and reflect on the work of others through the use of sharing feedback in the form of comments.

Digital Tool for Collaborating

www.voicethread.com   VoiceThread is a tool that allows multiple users to join into a shared discussion. It uses images, documents, and videos as a basis for conversations and allows users to respond using text, or audio or video recordings. This safe, secure site allows students an opportunity to collaborate on any subject imaginable. Teachers can use it to generate ideas for writing, reflect on texts, integrate content areas from other subjects, and promote higher-order thinking and critical analysis.

---

5. Consolidate: Digital tools provide countless opportunities for students to consolidate the learning that is happening in their classrooms and beyond. Learning is most powerful when students are able to apply it and transfer it to new situations. Creative applications allow students to consolidate their learning.

Digital Tools for Consolidating

Blogs provide a forum where writers can share ongoing reflections. Through this medium, students can consolidate and share their thoughts with others. While blogging is often considered a public form of reflection, there are platforms that allow students to blog in a safe, secure manner.

The Mirror
Sharing my reflections with my friends

Home   Sample Page

Feedback

Welcome!
Please share your feedback with me!

Categories
Uncategorized

Archives
February 2012

The Best Book I Ever Read
Posted on February 15, 2012

The best book I ever read was Poppy by Avi. I really loved the character Ereth. He is a grouchy porcupine who seems like such a grump. He will do anything for salt. He loves salt so much that he agrees to help Poppy so he can get some.

Mr. Ocax is an owl who tells the mice that he will protect them but he is really trying to scare them so he can eat them.

My favourite part is when Poppy meets Ereth. At first I was frightened that he would try to hurt her, but he is just tired and wants her to leave him alone.

Search

Recent posts
The Best Book I Ever Read

www.kidblog.org / www.edublog.org   Kidblog and Edublog are sites that provide forums for students to create and share blogs. They allow for teachers to monitor and control how blogs are published. Student blogs can be set to Private, ensuring that they are shared with only classmates and the teacher. Students are able to post their thoughts, reflections, stories, or any other form of work, and read and comment (or provide feedback) to their peers. The possibilities of student blogging are limitless. Blogs can be used as a vehicle for reflecting on reading, sharing writing pieces, or integrating learning from any other curriculum area.

---

6. Critically Analyze: As students encounter a broad range of texts, they need to be critically literate in order to analyze and evaluate the information they encounter. Because the Internet provides many opportunities to create and share content, users need to be ever more sceptical of the things they read. Students need to read information with a critical eye, considering the source of the information and the information itself in order to determine the reliability of the content.

The Media Triangle shown on page 144 is a framework that helps users understand and evaluate different texts. It takes into account the three faces of media (Text, Audience, and Production) and how they work together to create Meaning.

Text

- What form of media is this?
- How does the text attract the audience's attention?
- How does the text convey the message?
- What information is missing from the piece?

Audience

- What is the purpose of the piece?
- Who is the intended audience?
- How accurate do you think this message is?
- What does the message mean to you?
- Whose opinions are missing from the piece?
- What assumptions does the creator make about the intended audience?

Meaning

Production

- Who created the message? Why?
- How has the message been shared?
- Who does the message benefit?
- What techniques were used in the creation of the message?
- Are there any images, music, or elements that are used symbolically? Do they work effectively?

(Adapted from *A Guide To Effective Literacy Instruction: Media Literacy*, Ontario Ministry of Education, 2008: 39–40)

Tips for Tech Success

— Royan Lee

Writing a tip sheet for educators looking to integrate technology meaningfully into their programs is difficult for me to do. It's rather like trying to explain what my child looks and acts like to relatives overseas; in these exponential times, things could change at any moment. With this in mind, I nevertheless think it's important for any teacher working with technology in learning environments to consider three main questions.

First, why will you and your students use technology? The tools available these days (many of them free and web-based) can greatly complement, or even transform, anything you are trying to do around critical thinking, creativity, communication, or collaboration. But what, in *your* context, is the purpose? Are you trying to enhance student voice in your class? Do you want a more authentic audience for writing? Is it your hope that multiple intelligences and modalities will be honored in communication or understanding?

Secondly, what tools will help you accomplish your learning goals? For instance, if you're looking for a way for students to keep digital portfolios to foster reflection in the assessment process, a blog might be better than a learning management system like Moodle; the former gives more creative control to users than the latter. As another example, let's say you're looking for a tool to help you document observational and anecdotal assessment. A cloud-based note-taking tool, such as Evernote, could be far more useful for its portability and share-ability than a Word document on your laptop, which is cumbersome and tied to just one device. Connect your pedagogical purpose to the tool that fits.

And finally, how will you foster and maintain a collaborative inquiry-driven disposition? To have an environment where technology is embedded seamlessly into the learning that happens in your classroom and beyond, you're going to need to model and guide students with a growth mindset. This means you're going to discourage students from responding to technical issues (which will inevitably arise) in a reactionary, helpless manner. All problems and mistakes will be seen as learning opportunities.

With rich pedagogy and an inquiry disposition, you will be surprised how much your technological ambitions come to fruition.

Working with What You've Got

"I'll take 30 devices to go, please!" It's what digital dreams are made of! While we would love to have unlimited access to technology in our classes, the reality is that we all face challenges when it comes to resources. Perhaps you have a patchy wireless connection (or perhaps none at all) or struggle with filters that seem to restrict access to even the most harmless sites. Maybe you have a school lab that houses all the resources in one place or perhaps you have a set of devices stored on a portable cart that always seems to be in demand. Whatever the challenges you face, the solution comes with creativity and flexibility.

Integrating digital tools into a classroom is not as easy as introducing a new routine like independent reading or writing. It takes coordination and flexibility among teachers and students. There will be times when students are able to access more devices and times when the devices are completely unavailable for use. However, as with everything in literacy (and in life), we need to consider students' use and access to technology a part of a balancing act. It might not be possible for students to have unlimited access to devices at their beck and call but, by building in frequent opportunities for regular access and taking advantage of opportunities when students can access more devices than scheduled, we are able to incorporate digital tools as a part of balanced instruction throughout the year.

The 100 Minutes framework provides a way of incorporating technology into students' literacy experiences on a regular basis for about 40 minutes a day with as few as five or six devices. During AWARD Time, a Tech Time block can be designated for exclusive access by a group of students. While it might seem more practical to encourage students to use the devices for only half of the time and then allow another group to access them, the reality is that it often takes students a few minutes to get set up, log in, and access their work. If they are allowed the entire block of time (the entire AWARD Time), students are usually able to sink their teeth into a meaningful task and have enough time to make significant progress with it. With this model, students can have a designated Tech Time at least once a week, ensuring that they have sufficient time to make their experiences meaningful.

Guided Reading is another area of AWARD Time that teachers can use to incorporate digital tools and media literacy. Using devices as a text for discussion allows students to use their guided-reading time as a way of interacting with different forms of media. Including devices during guided reading allows for students of differing reading abilities to access the same text with ease. In this case, the term "text" can refer to any form of online media (including text, video, audio, and images). Finally, e-books include options of having text read aloud. Students can use headphones to access the information and engage in a discussion with their peers about content that might be above their independent reading levels.

Both Reading Time and Writing Time provide opportunities for teachers to use online text or digital tools as a way of integrating media and technology into students' daily learning experiences. With one computer and an LCD projector, teachers can access a wide range of texts and tools. They can use this time to model how to interpret and create different media texts while they are introducing students to tasks to work on during AWARD Time.

Regardless of how technology is present in the literacy block, it should always be an integrated component, intentionally connected to the learning that is happening in other areas. Technology should not be busy-work or a way of entertaining students. The time they spend engaged with digital tasks should be important and meaningful; it should allow them to extend and expand on their learning and not escape from their responsibilities. If we want students to be responsible with their use of technology, then it is our responsibility to provide them with learning tasks that are relevant and important. We need to constantly revisit the tasks, build on them throughout the year, and use technology as a way of enriching students' learning. Technology can be an incredibly valuable resource when used effectively. However, if not monitored and maintained, it has the potential to turn into a time when students are engaged and busy but not necessarily learning. Explicitly addressing the expectations for responsible technology use in the classroom, as well as providing rich tasks for students, will ensure that students' time is well-invested in supporting and expanding on their learning.

Kinetic Learning: Learning In Motion!

— at http://lisadonohue.wordpress.com/2012/02/16/kinetic-learning-learning-in-motion/

If metacognition is the "thinking about our thinking," what is the word that best describes our ability to *learn how to learn*? Learning in the 21st century means much more than being able to memorize content. It is more about the process of learning than the content of learning. But how do we begin to define this process of learning? It is certainly not a process that is static, but one that is always changing, a process that is evolving. Students need be able to access a range of learning strategies that allow them to be flexible when accessing, interpreting, and applying the information they need.

A discussion I had with Frieda Wishinsky resulted in the definition of a term for this new concept—*Kinetic Learning*. Frieda said:

> I believe that real learning is process. Learning has energy and motion. It's
> not facts. Facts come and go from your memory, but the how-to approach

develops, grows, and extends—not just into one subject but many. So much of testing kids has been about static knowledge rather than problem-solving. The more we let kids brainstorm, read widely, and learn how to learn, the better they will be at adapting to new situations and growing.

If we think of learning as having motion, a momentum that allows students to transfer the skills they learn in school to authentic real-life situations, it is truly kinetic. It is no longer about the potential that students have to gain and recall knowledge, but now about the power of applying their ability to learn in order to continue their learning.

Students can easily access content; therefore, learning in the 21st century can no longer be only about the acquisition of content. Instead we need to think of learning as a dynamic process in which we are teaching students, not only so that they will *learn*, but more importantly so that they will *become learners*.

Principles of Kinetic Learning
1. Kinetic Learning focuses on skills rather than content. In a world where information is easily accessible, students need to spend less time memorizing facts and more time learning how to access, interpret, analyze, and use the information they encounter.
2. Kinetic Learning is forward-thinking. It is not about the work they have done, but rather about the work they are going to do. Students need to be reflective learners, using feedback to set goals in order to help them transfer and apply their learning in new and novel situations.
3. Kinetic Learning is authentic and purposeful. Learning needs to be current, relevant, and important in the eyes of the students. Learners need to explicitly see the purpose for their learning and the value it will have in the future.
4. Kinetic Learning is multi-faceted. Learning is cross-curricular and incorporates skills from different disciplines. Through inquiry learning or collaborative problem-solving, students can apply a broad range of familiar strategies to explore new, unique, or interesting situations.
5. Kinetic Learning is Why- and How-based. Learning encourages students to think critically by challenging existing beliefs and to act collaboratively by expanding and building on the ideas of others.

Kinetic Learning is a dynamic process in which students learn valuable skills that will enable them to develop momentum in their learning. It is not about *learning knowledge* but rather the *knowledge of how to learn*. In the same way that meta-cognition is the process of thinking about our thinking, then Kinetic Learning is a process whereby we help students to learn how to learn. This is learning in motion!

Conclusion

If you're anything like me, when reading professional resources, you might stop reading too soon. It seems that once we have a handle on how something is going to work in our classrooms, we are so anxious to try it out that we assume we have gleaned sufficient information to just jump in. While that might be your initial impulse and you might be eager to start, there will come a time when establishing a routine is just not enough.

Good Routine Gone Bad

After my mom's death, my family started a new tradition. On Friday evenings the entire family would get together for Chinese food. It was a routine that everyone looked forward to. I remember telling colleagues that Fridays were now my favorite day, because not only did we get to spend time together as a family, but also it was one less day for which I needed to prepare a meal. My children looked forward to spending time with their grandfather and, truly, everyone savored our time together—not to mention the food. Friday after Friday, we arrived at my father's home for this shared meal. Initially this family routine was wonderful! It was great to gather together and we all felt that, despite our busy lives, it was good to know we would have dedicated family time on Fridays. With certainty, my father would purchase the Chinese food from his favorite local take-out. After a while he was on a first-name basis with the owner of the store and in no time at all he became a regular.

It wasn't long, however, before my children started to find excuses to miss our Friday family-night dinner. It started with my daughter not liking a certain kind of chicken, then my son (who eats virtually anything) reluctantly pushing his food around his plate. Gradually, we all started to lose interest in our Friday-night Chinese-food feast.

While we all thoroughly enjoyed spending time together, the food selection had grown boring. It was not the routine that was the problem, but the content. The food that not long ago was a favorite of all had somehow lost its appeal. The predictability and regularity caused us to lose interest. Was it that we no longer wanted to have a family meal every week? No. But the lack of variety and choice resulted in a feeling of monotony. Gradually, the Friday-night family Chinese-food routine lost its place in our lives.

Once the routine was established, it needed to continue to grow, continue to develop, and respond to the interest and needs of the different family members. I'm certain that, had we had varied the food choices and considered the preferences of everyone involved, the Friday-night family routine would have been much more long-lived.

While routines are necessary for getting things started, the simple establishment of a routine is not sufficient to keep it going. All routines need maintenance. They need to be revisited, tweaked, and strengthened. They need to reflect the needs and interests of the participants, and to include opportunities for them to express their choices.

A Different Kind of Family Meal

This book is the "family restaurant" of my literacy experiences: if you dine at a family restaurant, you might find they serve a gravy recipe they got from their great-aunt Mildred with Grandpa Joe's traditional roast beef, or perhaps a mint jelly recipe they found in a cookbook with their sister's style of making lamb chops. Through the years, I have gathered countless ideas from a plethora of sources: teachers, friends, colleagues, books, professional development sessions, various courses. Although I've done my best to track down the sources of my inspirations, there might be instances where someone has been missed. If this is the case, please forgive me. As with the family restaurant, after a while all the delicious recipes seem to blend together into the chef's repertoire and the original source may be lost. Teaching, as with cooking, is about collecting recipes for success and then refining them into a way that works best for you. It is truly synthesis in action. We take the things we learn and find new and creative ways of bringing them into our classes; somewhere in that mix, they become our own. I hope that by sharing a part of your literacy journey with me, you'll be able to take some of the ideas from this book and make them your own.

Bibliography

Allen, J. (2002) *On the Same Page: Shared reading beyond the primary grades.* Portland, ME: Stenhouse.

Allington, R. (2002) "What I've Learned about Effective Reading Instruction" *Phi Delta Kappan*: 740–747.

Amosa, W., Williams, C., Ladwig, J.G., Gore, J.M. & Griffiths, T. (2008) "An Examination of the Quality and Conceptualisation of English Teaching." Paper presented at the *Australian Association for Research in Education Annual Conference.*

Atwell, N. (2003) *In the Middle: New understandings about writing, reading and learning* (2nd ed.). Portsmouth, NH: Boynton/Cook.

Bereiter, C. & Scardamalia, M. (1987) *The Psychology of Written Composition.* Hillsdale, NJ: Heinemann.

Brand, M. (2004) *Word Savvy: Integrated vocabulary, spelling and word study, grades 3–6.* Portland, ME: Stenhouse.

Boushey, G. & Moser, J. (2006) *The Daily 5: Fostering literacy independence in the elementary grades.* Portland, ME: Stenhouse

Brookhart, S. (2008) "Feedback" *Educational Leadership*, December 2007/ January 2008, Association for Supervision and Curriculum Development.

Cunningham, P.M. & Allington, R.L. (2003) *Classrooms That Work: They can all read and write* (3rd ed.) New York, NY: Allyn & Bacon.

Clarke, S. (2003) *Enriching Feedback in the Primary Classroom.* London, UK: Hodder & Stoughton.

Daniels, H. (2002) *Literature Circles: Voice and choice in book club and reading groups.* Markham, ON: Pembroke.

Davies, Anne (2008) *Leading the Way to Making Classroom Assessment Work.* Courtenay, BC: Connections Publishing.

— (2008) *Transforming Barriers to Assessment for Learning.* Courtenay, BC: Connections Publishing.

Donohue, L. (2008) *Independent Reading Inside the Box.* Markham, ON: Pembroke.

— (2009) *The Write Beginning.* Markham, ON: Pembroke.

— (2010) *Keepin' It Real.* Markham, ON: Pembroke.

— (2011) *The Write Voice.* Markham, ON: Pembroke.

Earle, L.M. (2003) *Assessment As Learning, Using classroom assessment for learning.* Courtenay, BC: Connections Publishing.

Fountas, I.C. &Pinnell, S.G. (2001) *Guiding Readers and Writers, Grades 3-6: Teaching comprehension, genre and content literacy.* Portsmouth, NH: Heinemann.

Harvey, S. & Goudvis, A. (2000/2007) *Strategies That Work: Teaching comprehension for understanding and engagement*. Portland, ME: Stenhouse.

Hillcocks, G. (1995) *Teaching Writing as Reflective Practice*. New York: Teachers College Press.

Houtveen, A. A. M & van de Grift, W. J. C. M. (2007) "Effects of Metacognitive Strategy Instruction and Instruction Time on Reading Comprehension" in *School Effectiveness and School Improvement*, Volume 18, Issue 2: 173–190.

Mooney, M. (1990) *Reading To, With, and By Children*. Katonah, NY: Richard C. Owen.

Ontario Ministry of Education (2004) *Literacy for Learning: The report of the Expert Panel on Literacy in grades 4 to 6 in Ontario*.

— (2006/2008) *A Guide to Effective Literacy Instruction: Grade 4–6* Volumes 2–7: (Assessment, Planning and Classroom Management, Oral Language, Reading, Writing, Media Literacy).

— (2006) *The Ontario Curriculum Grades 1–8: Language*.

Parr, M. & Campbell, T. (2012) *Balanced Literacy Essentials: Weaving theory into practice for successful instruction in reading, writing and talk*. Markham, ON: Pembroke

Pressley, M. (2000) "What Should Comprehension Instruction be the Instruction of?" cited in Barr, R., Pearson, D., Kamil, M.L. & Mosenthal, P., *Handbook of Reading Research*. Marhwah, NJ: Lawrence Erlbaum.

Routman, R. (2005) *Writing Essentials: Raising expectations and results while simplifying teaching*. Portsmouth, NH: Heinemann.

Scott, R.M. & Siamon, S. (2004) *Spelling: Connecting the pieces*. Toronto, ON: Gage Learning.

Spiegel, D.L. (2005) *Classroom Discussion*. New York, NY: Scholastic

Tierney, R. & Pearson, D. (1992) "A revisionist perspective on 'Learning to learn from text: A framework for improving classroom practice'" in Ruddell, R.B., Ruddell, M.R. & Singer, H. (Eds.) *Theoretical models and processes of reading* (4th ed.). Newark, DE: International Reading Association.

Wood, D.E. (2006) "Modeling the Relationship Between Oral Reading Fluency and Performance on a Statewide Reading Test" *Educational Assessment*, Volume 11, Issue 2: 85–104.

Woolley, G. (2007) "A Comprehension Intervention for Children with Comprehension Difficulties" *Australian Journal of Learning Disabilities*, Volume 12, Issue 1: 43–50.

Index